THE BOOK OF
matchbox labels

ROGER FENNINGS

New Cavendish Books

First published in UK by New Cavendish Books
November 2001

Publisher: Narisa Chakra
Design: Supadee Ruangsak
Photography: Luke Kelly

All items illustrated are from the author's collection.

ISBN: 1 872727 24 7

Printed and bound in Thailand by
Amarin Printing and Publishing (Plc.) Co.,Ltd.

New Cavendish Books
3 Denbigh Road
London W11 2SJ
Tel. 020 77929984, 72296765
Fax. 020 77920027
E-mail: narisa@new-cav.demon.co.uk
www.newcavendishbooks.com

Contents

Introduction

The matchbox label is full of surprises. This Swedish label from the 1890s (opposite page), shows one of the company's products used as a miniature Punch and Judy theatre. The more modern label from Czechoslovakia starts us on a fascinating journey through time and design.

Have you got a light? Take a look in your pocket, handbag, glove compartment, kitchen or office drawer and the chances are you'll find a box of matches.

It's not so long ago that a simple box of matches was something no-one could be without.

In today's world it would be fair to say that the need for a box of matches is increasingly being displaced by disposable (and wasteful) lighters, electric cookers, gas stoves with electronic ignition, central heating rather than open fires – and a decline in smoking.

But in less developed and highly-populated regions of Africa, South America, the Indian sub-continent and China, the use of matches in domestic cooking, heating and lighting remains all-important. And in countries where smoking is on the increase and even the simplest lighter is an unattainable luxury, the smoker needs matches.

How is it then that the matchbox, virtually indispensable for almost two centuries and familiar to everyone, is so undervalued and unrecognised? Why are their labels, so varied, colourful and informative, are not acknowledged for what they are – a fascinating source of social history and graphic design? Probably because their simple practicality has rendered them mundane, to be thrown away after use, ironically just like the disposable lighters which are increasingly usurping the box of matches.

Cheap, easily available, produced by the million, most matchboxes get discarded when empty, along with their labels. Yet the history of the match, the match industry and those that helped build it has been preserved by a handful of the major manufacturers, although many are now defunct.

Matches have been produced and sold in countless different forms and packages. Here we shall focus on the matchbox label and its many messages. What we hope this book will bring is an insight to the creativity, diversity and imagination that has been applied all over the world to using the matchbox label not only as a source of information and education – but also, as a cultural kaleidoscope and a treasure chest for collectors.

Hopefully, after looking through these pages, you will see the matchbox in a new light.

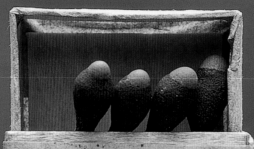

BRYANT & MAY'S

BRAIDED

CICAR LICHTS

HEADS CANNOT FALL OFF

"BRYMAY" SAFETY MATCHES

6

Chapter One

The First Matches

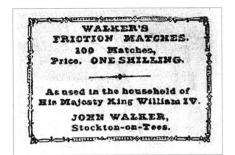

Was this the first Matchbox Label? Reproduction of John Walker's first box.

This pair may make a good match but in reality would never have been seen together. The Braided Cigar lights from 1865 pre-date the Minton matchbox holder and ashtray by some 70 years.

Never mind rubbing two sticks together, concentrating the sun's rays onto a heap of kindling through a bit of glass or banging bits of flint together in the hope of making a spark; striking a light was difficult enough even after the invention of the first rudimentary matches.

It's hard to know who to give the credit – or the blame – for the earliest marriages of stick or splint with mixtures of chemicals of varying volatility which, when introduced to an abrasive surface, caused a small – and usually smelly – detonation.

Some say it was the Chinese, famous for their pyrotechnic abilities, while others have different opinions, but whatever the source of inspiration today's safety matches were preceded by several centuries of ingenuity which spawned matches that would ignite spontaneously on contact with air, (and were consequently hard to extinguish), and others that would only do so when dipped in sulphuric acid. Some had glass or ceramic stems, most were wax or wood with a head designed to strike on a rough surface, such as a brick, a piece of sandpaper or the sole of a boot.

Early matches were sold loose, wrapped in paper, with the potential to ignite against each other. Some came with a separate abrasive striking strip, while some even had their heads braided to the stems by a thread, preventing them from flying off and igniting the wrong target when struck. Stories that the little leather patch on the back of a pair of jeans was originally placed there to enable the striking of non-safety matches seem to be without foundation.

Public places such as cafes and hotels provided glass, ceramic or metal holders with rough surfaces for patrons to strike their matches on – now highly collectable items in themselves – and the better-off had their own fancy silver vesta cases to carry their matches in, and these too are in high demand by collectors.

So it came as something of a blessing when the forerunner of the match as we know it today first went on sale in 1827. These 'friction lights' – matches that would only strike on their own specially-prepared surface - were the result of a chance experiment the previous year by the English chemist John Walker, and within a few years phosphorous-based friction matches were being widely sold by a proliferation of small factories.

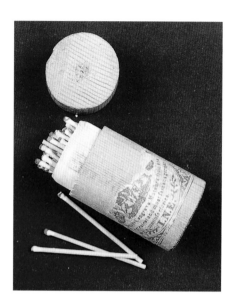

A handwritten inscription on the back of this cylinder of sulphur matches (above), made by J.N.Engert of Nuremberg, records that it was part of the last shipment of these matches to Australia, in 1847. Although the label is damaged the annotation on the back adds interest. Despite their fragility, a surprising number of old matchboxes survive in good condition. Right: an early box from the Italian de Medici factory.

But the dangerous, toxic phosphorous was an increasing cause of contention among users; housewives and smokers alike found the noxious fumes given off by these devices to be intolerable, and those that hand-made the matches suffered the sometimes fatal consequences of ingesting poisonous chemicals.

It wasn't until the mid 1850s that a phosphorous-free match worthy of the name 'safety match' was produced. It was to ignite a huge explosion in the demand for, and production of, matches, matches properly packed in boxes providing both container and integral striking surface.

Hot competition

The proliferation in the manufacture and sale of matches was rapid, and hot competition broke out among those emulating Walker's formula, and seeking to improve upon it.

The real breakthrough came in 1855 when the first non-toxic red phosphorous – based safety matches became available, thanks to the ingenuity of Swedes Johan Edvard Lundström and Arvid Sjöberg.

Within a decade the production of these, the forerunners of today's safety matches, was widespread throughout Europe, with factories springing up to meet demand. Some of them were to disappear quickly, victims to the fre-

quent fires and explosions that beset the industry, destroying lives, businesses, and historical records. But those that survived went from strength to strength, amalgamated and merged and formed some of the world's most important conglomerates.

Since those early days matches have been offered in boxes and packages of every conceivable shape and size. In the beginning they were often sold loose, sometimes wrapped in a twist of paper, sometimes in a paper banderole, sometimes in wooden or card pillboxes known as capsules, often without a label. Again, it was probably the Swedes who introduced the first matchboxes as we now know them today, when J.S.Bagge, credited with establishing the first match factory in Sweden in 1836, introduced them a few years later.

While credit for the invention of the first phosphorous matches may go variously to a trio of Frenchmen, namely Chancel (1805), Francois Derosne (1816) or Charles Sauria, who in 1831 had produced the only usable, but poisonous, sulphur match, it was John Walker's spark of genius that launched the modern match with its box and safe striker.

Once the public recognised the value of Johan Lundström's improved formula for a friction match that would only strike on a special surface, without the usual toxic fumes, demand increased dramatically. And when Lundström sold the British patent, in 1855, to William Bryant and Francis May, the foundations were laid for the growth of a company that was to become one of the world's major match manufacturers: Bryant & May, whose 'Brymay' brand was literally – and actually – to become a household name.

To meet demand, Britain was at this time importing matches from Austria and Germany, as well as Sweden. Now the market could be locally supplied. Meanwhile match factories were going into increased production in Austria and Germany. The French continued to produce volumes of phosphorous matches, and in Italy the Albani factory, established in 1833, was gaining ground. The Lavaggi company, although estab-

lished later, in 1845, was by this time already exporting substantial quantities of matches to neighbouring countries, including Albania, Egypt and Turkey, and it too was to grow to become an important enterprise. But the most important factories in Italy were probably those of Giacomo de Medici, in Milan and Magenta, and his son Luigi in Turin.

The first factory to be established in Belgium was set up by Balthazar Mertens in Lessines and was operational by 1835. In Norway, some fifty different factories were in production between 1846 and 1900, but only seven were to survive the turn of the century. Spain was to witness equally rapid growth; Pascasio Lizarbe Ruiz opened his factory in 1840, and by 1892 fifty-four more had opened for him to compete with.

Supplies of good quality timber were important to match makers, so where forests of the preferred timber, pine or aspen, flourished, so did the match industry. Scandinavia, Finland, Austria, Germany, Belgium and most of the East European states were all blessed with the raw materials to help them develop local match industries that would grow and to dominate global match markets, and those companies were the ones that survived the longest.

The earliest matchbox labels were short on design and economical with words. The top label, on a cylindrical box from Sweden's Jönköping factory, could be the world's smallest at 9mmx18mm and dates from about 1848. The one below, of similar vintage, simply states 'Jönköpings cigar lights'.

Despite intense competition, it was Sweden that would emerge as the major force in match production. In 1917 the union of all Swedish manufacturers created one giant company – Swedish Match – which brought together 18 separate factories.

Some years earlier, in 1903, a similar merger in Austria created an equally powerful competitor – Solo.

After its foundation, Swedish Match soon saw rapid growth and foreign expansion, taking over competitors in other Scandinavian countries, in Belgium, Germany, Holland, Austria and Hungary and entering into joint ventures of various types in Britain, Spain, Greece, Poland, France and USA.

In India there was an almost insatiable demand for matches and, with little local expertise, this was initially met by imports. Soon, however, a vast cottage industry had sprung up and match producers proliferated, with government encouragement. In 1923 Swedish Match established itself in India in the shape of WIMCO, which continued to flourish through the 1950s, when once again growth was slowed by the government's renewed support of local enterprise.

The global spread of Swedish Match was fuelled by growing demand and lack of reliable raw materials – timber for the splints and sophisticated chemicals – in some of the world's biggest match markets. In Africa, Asia and South America difficult climatic conditions did nothing to facilitate production of safe matches without considerable expertise, although the pyrotechnic ability of Chinese and Japanese manufacturers saw rapid, if unsophisticated, progress towards the development of a new industry that was to compete strongly with European factories.

Britain's Bryant & May was also enjoying rapid expansion. An amalgamation with the American company Diamond Match embraced ownership of the Irish Match Company and interests in South Africa which, with the bringing together of all that country's factories in 1905, saw the creation of the Lion Match Company. Interests in Australia and New Zealand were acquired soon after.

Bryant & May and Swedish Match continued to grow and diversify, each acquiring interests in the production of card, chemicals, forestry and even disposable lighters: logical business strategy in the interest of sustaining production and market share.

Eventually, inevitably, they were to come together when, in 1987, Swedish Match took over Wilkinson Sword, with whom Bryant & May had merged in 1973. In 1994 Swedish Match closed the Bryant & May factory and in 1997 ceased trading using the last Bryant & May name. Today, Swedish Match remains the world's leading match manufacturer.

Safer than carrying matches loose or wrapped in paper, and more stylish, silver vesta cases were popular at the time. This one (left), was made in Birmingham in 1898. Match companies also offered their own tins, like these from the Diamond Match Co. of America, dated 1880 (below left), and the 1868 'Sportsman' made by Bryant & May.

Chapter Two

Matchbox Messages

Modern matchboxes carry an astonishing and colourful variety of messages and images on their labels. But this was certainly not the case in the early days.

Back in 1827 John Walker's first matches were sold in plain tins of 100 splints. Others were sold loose, tied with string, or in plain paper wrappers. With no real trade mark laws coming into place until the 1880s, and little competition, branding as we now know it was in its infancy; commercial artwork hardly existed, particularly in the match industry.

Most imagery was decorative rather than promotional, and attempted to beautify mundane objects rather than publicise them.

This situation was to change very rapidly with the industrial revolution and the explosive development of the match industry and the many factories that sprang up as a result. Just how many factories were established in those first boom years is hard to know, as many were little more than family-run cottage industries – and many records were destroyed by the frequent fires that were associated with match manufacture.

By 1860 there were about 30 factories in London alone, while in Sweden there were some 170. And as manufacturers in Europe and further afield took up the challenge of meeting the increasing demand for the new matches, copied techniques and wrangled over licenses and patents, the need for clearer identity to protect the just initiators of the booming new business was quickly apparent.

Even when manufacturers did start identifying themselves and their products they tended to be economical with the wording. One of the earliest, and probably the world's smallest matchbox label, measuring just 9mm x 18mm, simply says 'Jönköping's Cigartändare', identifying the 'cigar lights' as made by the Jönköping factory of Sweden. The labels were attached to paper 'banderole' wrappers (sometimes replaced by a simple rubber stamp), or to thin matchwood pillboxes.

Jönköping produced a number of equally tersely-worded labels between the mid 1840s and early 1850s, although they began to acquire decorative borders and increase in size. Other Swedish manufacturers soon followed suit, as did their counterparts around the world.

Mr. Pojatzi was not shy to advertise his matches on this early Austrian label, (left), while the Swedish label above devotes its message to safety.

THE.SAFETY.MATCHS.

厚記洋行　厚記洋行

TRADE　MARK

KOYEKISHA.TOKIO.JAPAN.

Early Japanese labels were always colourful, sometimes crude.

With competition intensifying in the rapidly growing match industry – particularly in Europe – match makers soon realised that they needed to do more than just put their name on the matchbox. They had to sell the benefits of their own brands over others to an increasingly discerning public, who had for long enough endured the problems of poor quality, dangerous or difficult-to-light matches, and who quite literally, didn't want to keep getting their fingers burnt.

There was an equally urgent need to alert users of the new matches as to how to handle and use them safely. A simple action which is so familiar to us today was a novelty then. A label

on an early German box described the process: "These matches must, as the above drawing shows, be taken between the fingers, and the box, being previously shut again, they may be instantly ignited by softly rubbing against the bottom of the box itself, although the same effect is produced by softly rubbing them against any other hard substance."

Other messages were more straightforward. "Rub lightly on a small part of the prepared surface" implored Messrs. Bryant & May, and "strike the tip gently".

But what about the competitive edge? Whose matches were best? Were safety matches, in other words those that only ignited on a specially-prepared surface, preferable or more practical than the 'strike anywhere' kind?

Initially, Bryant & May seemed ambivalent. 'Strike anywhere', they proclaimed on their imported matches in the 1850s, while 'Protection from Fire' was to become their sales slogan of the future. Their Flaming Fusees promised to 'flame in wind or rain'. Their Congreve Lights were 'warranted suitable for any climate', while their Safety Fusees were 'the only light that can be carried in the pocket with safety'.

A Swedish brand of the same era described itself as a 'triumph of science', adding that 'the wood of

An early proof of the famous Bryant & May 'Ark' label, dated 25 August 1910, is strong on safety instructions, while 'The Zebra' (left), from Sweden's Mönsterås Kalmar factory claimed to be 'the safest in the world' in 1912. The Japanese offered matches that were 'watertight', 'without comparison in the world' and 'guaranteed the not damps'.

Safety claims from Sweden in 1896 (left), Japan, and a rare 1898 example from America's Diamond Match Co.

each match is chemically treated so that the glowing portion of wood never falls off (NB: a fruitful cause of disastrous or fatal fires). Wonderfully interesting discovery. Try it!'

Strong words indeed. But it was to be Jönköpings subtle 'Ignites only on the box' that became the enduring – and much copied – catchphrase of the future.

In 1898 America's Diamond Match Company produced a brand whose pink box announced that 'the Press Match has a fire-proof handle for safety. Will not glow. Leaves no embers. Cannot burn the fingers. Comes in and goes out at the proper time.' – whenever that was.

And let us not forget the Japanese, eager to capitalise on the trend and secure for themselves a lucrative piece of the local market, hitherto dominated by imports.

'This match emits no bad smell, can strike anywhere and is extra useful', said a label on a box manufactured by Kobayashi of Kobe.

In 1885 the Naoki factory claimed their matches to be 'without comparison in the world'.

Shiyojukan of Osaka meanwhile were producing what they described as 'watertight' (rather than waterproof) matches, while the Kita factory of Hiogo topped the lot by proudly proclaiming that their Choice Choice Registered Elephant Brand matches were 'guaranteed the not damps'!

Even the recalcitrant Mr. Walker, who started the whole thing, was obliged to announce on the first labels he produced for his friction matches (one shilling for 100) that they were 'as used in the household of His Majesty King William IV'.

But sterner stuff was to come. Plagiarism and copying of trademarks was finally doomed when Bryant & May were able to legally register their Noah's Ark emblem by Royal Letters Patent in 1872, and even produced a label saying so. 'Fraud' it said; 'Without taking the precaution of observing closely the name Bryant & May and trade mark (an Ark) the Public may be imposed upon with an article that does not afford Protection from Fire'.

That trade mark remains famous to this day. And the matchbox label was beginning to take on a significance all of its own.

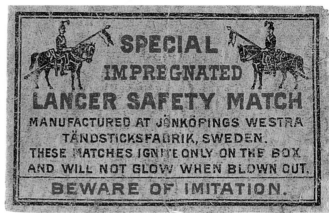

IMPREGNATED SAFETY

C·W·S

PACKET TEAS

ARE

REFRESHING TO THE **BRAIN-WORKER**

AND

SOOTHING TO THE TOILER

MATCHES MADE IN SWEDEN

SPECIAL
IMPREGNATED
LANCER SAFETY MATCH
MANUFACTURED AT JÖNKÖPINGS WESTRA
TÄNDSTICKSFABRIK, SWEDEN.
THESE MATCHES IGNITE ONLY ON THE BOX
AND WILL NOT GLOW WHEN BLOWN OUT.
BEWARE OF IMITATION.

SPECIAL
LION SAFETY MATCHES.
Manufactured at ÖREBRO Sweden.
These matches do not glow when
extinguished nor do the ends drop off.
BEWARE OF IMITATION.

THESE SPECIAL PATENT MATCHES
ARE MADE IN SWEDEN
WITHOUT PHOSPHORUS
FROM GLOWLESS WOOD
BEING IMPREGNATED THEY CEASE
TO GLOW
AFTER THE FLAME IS EXTINGUISHED
BEWARE OF INFERIOR MATCHES

*Early matchbox messages
like these from the 1890s
concentrated on safety, then
opened up to advertising.*

**NONPAREIL
INDIAN " CHUTNEY ".
DELICIOUS! DIGESTIVE!
SOLE MANUFACTURER
EDWD MANWARING
PECKHAM LONDON S.E.
MATCHES MADE IN SWEDEN.**

THE RUNAWAY MATCH

SOLE MANUFACTURERS
BRYANT & MAY
LONDON.

ENTERED AT STATIONERS HALL

1 x

Chapter Three

To Communicate Or Decorate

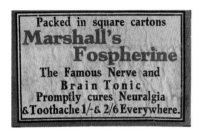

Packed in square cartons
Marshall's
Fospherine
The Famous Nerve and
Brain Tonic
Promptly cures Neuralgia
& Toothache 1/- & 2/6 Everywhere.

Decorative labels like Bryant & May's 'Runaway' of the 1880s contrasted sharply with later advertising labels.

By the late nineteenth century the simple matchbox with its safe and easy-to-use contents was commonplace almost all over the world, thanks to high demand, rapid development and the increasingly competitive battle for export markets and local manufacturing licenses.

The need for elaborate instructions on how to use or strike a match became redundant. Manufacturers now had to direct their matchbox messages to audiences that were highly diverse economically, politically and ethnically. They had to deliver their own competitive sales messages and brand image as well as meet a customer demand for boxes that were attractive and decorative too. Fashionable European ladies, for example, liked to use them in their drawing rooms as much as the head of the household in a remote African village needed them to light the fire beneath the family cooking pot.

In undeveloped nations where illiteracy was high, communication had to be pictorial rather than wordy. This in turn meant that European manufacturers seeking to penetrate African or Asian markets needed to be aware of local tastes and taboos, where depicting the wrong kind of

animal or plant could have far-reaching effects.

All of this created something of a challenge to manufacturers, who found themselves having to get the most possible impact out of a space that comprised at most a couple of panels of about 40 x 60mm.

The resulting imagination and ingenuity put into this by manufacturers, importers and distributors large and small gave birth to a variety of themes and images probably unequalled by any other type of consumer packaging.

In Britain, names such as Bryant & May, Moreland & Sons, Maguire & Paterson, J.Palmer and J.John Masters were rapidly becoming familiar. Of the many Swedish companies Jönköping and Vulcan quickly gained prominence. In the United States, which had almost 150 factories in the latter part of the 19th century, the Diamond, Universal and Ohio match companies were to dominate, while in Canada the Eddy Match Co. was almost unrivalled. Other names to establish themselves were to be Pojatzi, B.Fürth and Solo in Austria; Union Match in Belgium; Lion and Rosebank in South Africa; H.E.Gosch in Denmark; Nitedals in Norway; the

Simple and effective messages for Bernard Fürth's Austrian matches and (opposite), soap powder and purifying pills.

various factories of Messrs.Kolbe and Pohl in Zanow, Germany – and countless others in Europe, India, Japan and Africa. All sought to establish themselves, their names and brands, be they independent enterprise or government monopoly.

Rarely has such a simple day-to-day necessity generated so much global activity, employment, competition and controversy as the box of matches in its emerging years.

It would not be too long before the matchbox label in its many forms was to become a new hunting ground for collectors, which in turn was to stimulate manufacturers to cater for this additional market. But before this the matchbox label had to go through a lengthy evolutionary process in establishing its various roles, including message carrier and advertising medium.

Gradually the shape and size of the boxes – and their contents – began to be more uniform, and with the box of safety matches now established as the cheap, efficient and

modern way of making fire, the labels had to do the selling.

Even by the turn of the century the manufacture of matches and matchboxes was relatively crude and used a combination of machinery and manual labour. But once those early machines were refined and continuous production methods introduced and developed, the match industry was to represent one of the most highly mechanised and efficient manufacturing processes in the world: a far cry from the early days of cottage industry, child labour, dispute and disease. The notorious 'phossy jaw', a necrosis which caused the breakdown of tissue in match workers' jawbones, was to claim many young lives.

Meanwhile, the all-round-the-box label was an integral part of matchbox manufacture during the competition for customers. The paper label was wrapped right around the box and served to hold together the thin wood of the box sleeve. Once secured, the striking surface compound was painted on one, or both, sides. Frequently, however, it was only applied on one side, leaving the top, bottom and one side panel to be printed with manufacturers' – or advertisers' – messages.

Manufacturers began offering the back panels of their all-round-the-box labels to advertisers, and the ever-innovative Bryant & May were among the first to develop this business. Before long, British matchboxes were carrying advertisements for candles, gin, disinfectant, soap, sunflower oil, cigarettes, tobacco, pipes, and many other necessities of life, including Hinkley's Celebrated Cordial Powders for Horses and Marshall's Famous Fospherine Nerve and Brain Tonic. In other parts of Europe, and in the United States, similar commercial opportunities were being recognised and taken. The commercial exploitation of the box of matches, its contents and its label, was taking off.

With the public now well educated in the etiquette of match handling, those lengthy safety instructions were no longer necessary. So as long as the all-round-the-box label continued to be used, manufacturers tended to want to put something on them rather than leave blank panels. To start with this was usually a double-sided version of their brand or trademark, which naturally enough helped multiply awareness of their product. But it was not long before more and more variety and colour was to appear.

Labels began to be produced with decorative designs and patterns on the bottom and side and even the top panels become more pictorial and more attractive. Topical and seasonal subjects, historical events, personalities and anniversaries were popular themes of the time, particularly in Europe. Soon these same themes were being adapted to overseas markets too. All over the world, as match makers saw production and consumption increase apace, they were unanimous in recognising the potential of the matchbox as a source of advertising revenue, and the still varied methods of production and non-standard sizes of boxes provided producers some flexibility in this respect.

By the early twentieth century the matchbox was to change. Machinery and manufacturing processes became more refined, and as established manufacturers in Britain, Scandinavia, Eastern Europe and the USA expanded and acquired smaller companies and factories in new markets further afield, so production techniques and the products themselves became more standardised. Machinery then introduced – initially developed in Sweden but soon to be of mainly German origin – enabled the continuous process to evolve. This meant that the thin wood for the matchbox sleeve was cut, folded, and bound into shape by a paper wrapper (usually blue). The inner tray was similarly folded and glued, and its contents inserted by the filling machine. With the striking surfaces painted onto the box, sleeve and tray were married and the label glued on top. The all-round-the-box label virtually disappeared. The size of the matchbox and its contents became much more uniform around the world – while the matchbox label exploded into diversity as a means to communicate, educate, decorate and commemorate.

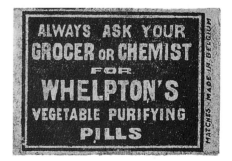

TRADE MARK.

ENT^D AT STA HALL.

BRYANT & MAY

LONDON.

TRADE   MARK.

Chapter Four

Birth of the World's Biggest Brands

Bryant & May's 1876 'Tiger' brand may be more colourful but their 'Ark' trademark was to become one of the world's most enduring.

In some parts of the world, that 'new' machinery is still functioning, reliable as ever, and many of the brands they were serving then are still with us today. Some have changed a little over the years, as have tastes and styles, most are under new ownership, but many of the world's biggest brands have become a familiar part of daily life and, in various forms, have survived the best part of a century.

The great survivors among British brands include Bryant & May's Brymay Ark, 'England's Glory', 'Scottish Bluebell', 'Bo Peep', 'Swift', and, probably most famous of all, Swan, the 'smoker's match'. The swan swam to the left for many years, but changed direction in 1959. 'Tiger' and 'Capt. Webb' were also firm favourites, the latter to commemorate the captain's remarkable achievement of becoming, in 1875, the first person to swim the English Channel. The matchbox label outlived the captain by many years.

The variety and quality of labels to come from Sweden is legendary, and key brands from the various factories that comprise today's Swedish Match enterprise are famous all over the world. Probably the most ubiquitous, in its numerous subtle forms, is Jönköpings Original, a relatively unremarkable black-on-yellow label bearing the bold 'Säkerhets-Tändstickor' (safety matches) wavy headline and four prize medals.

It was to be a design that was frequently and flagrantly copied – probably because it was so simple – yet which was to become a global symbol of good quality safety matches. Possibly the biggest seller of all is the Solstickan (Sun Match) brand, whose label bears the curly-headed, bare-bottomed, toddler that represents a huge contribution of funds to help disabled and under-privileged children and old people.

Other globally-recognised Swedish brands include 'The Ship', whose three-masted clipper, flying the Swedish flag, has appeared in numerous varieties over the years, 'Three Stars', 'Flower Basket', (still dominant in the Middle East), and the Uddevalla factory's 'Swallow'.

The flame-haired ladies on Australia's 'Redheads' label instantly evoke the red-headed matches their boxes contain, while in neighbouring New Zealand the 'Beehive' brand

Bryant & May's 'Tiger' was to be outlived by the Swedish Match 'Ship'.

THE SMOKER'S MATCH

SWAN VESTAS

BRYANT & MAY LTD.
BRITISH MADE

SWAN VESTAS

SPECIALLY MADE FOR SMOKERS.
WHITE WOOD OF THE FINEST QUALITY.
ARE BRITISH AND BEST.
NEVER SPOIL THE FLAVOUR OF
THE TOBACCO.

SWAN VESTAS
SPECIALLY MADE FOR SMOKERS.
WHITE PINE OF THE FINEST QUALITY.
ARE BRITISH AND BEST.
NEVER SPOIL THE FLAVOUR OF THE TOBACCO.

BRYANT & MAY LTD.
LONDON, LIVERPOOL, GLASGOW & LEEDS.

THE SMOKER'S MATCH

SWAN VESTAS

BRITISH MADE

WHITE PINE VESTAS
THE SWAN TRADE MARK
MADE BY THE ROSEBANK MATCH Cº LD

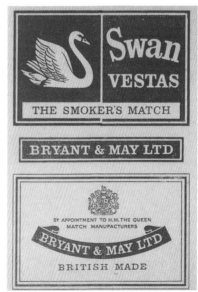

Swan VESTAS

THE SMOKER'S MATCH

BRYANT & MAY LTD

BY APPOINTMENT TO H.M. THE QUEEN
MATCH MANUFACTURERS

BRYANT & MAY LTD

BRITISH MADE

Various versions of the famous 'Swan Vestas' brand, which first appeared in 1883. The Swan White Pine Vestas were produced by the Rosebank Match Co. of South Africa in about 1903. In 1959 the swan changed direction and swam to the right, and continues to do so on today's modern 'Swan Vestas' box.

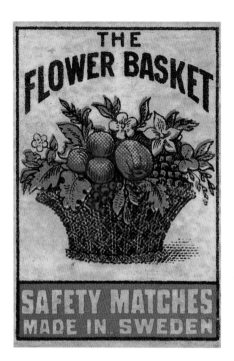

the Fiat Lux factory that issued it.

Czechoslovakia's Solo Match Works was to become one of Eastern Europe's major producers, issuing several export brands that remain familiar all over the world, including 'The Scissors' and 'The Key'.

The best-known label from France is almost certainly the rather plain red and white 'Allumettes de Sûreté' design for the French State Monopoly, produced in many factories over many years, while Heinrich Schmidt's design for Germany's blue-and-white World Matches ('Welt-Hölzer') also had remarkable staying power. Interestingly, many of the longest-lived labels have very simple designs.

No-one could ever count the number of different labels produced by India's numerous factories, large and small, but it is probably WIMCO's much-copied 'Horse Head' brand that takes the honours for being best known.

Appropriately enough Holland's 'Molen' (windmill) brand kept sales turning over nicely for many years, while South Africa's Lion Match Co.'s 'Lion', first recorded in 1882, must be a contender for one of the longest-running of all. 'Independence', 'Ohio Blue Tip' and 'Diamond' still fly the flag for the USA.

An ark, a ship, a bluebell, a flower basket, a swan, a swallow and a swift; a humming bird, a horses' head, a beehive and a tent. All these images made their mark for match makers world wide – and that was just the beginning.

represents the quality customers have come to expect from Bryant & May, Bell & Co., a relationship established by Bryant & May in 1908

One of the most prolific producers of the era was Belgium, whose numerous factories turned out countless attractive labels, many of which have withstood the test of time, including the Union Match Co.'s 'Three Torches' in all its many forms, and the ubiquitous 'Camp' brand. Brazil's 'Beija-Flor' (humming bird) was another strong survivor, as was

'Flower Basket' and 'Scissors': famous brands from Sweden and Czechoslovakia.

Sweden's 'Three Stars' brand is one of the world's best-recognised. 'The Key', from Czechoslovakia's Solo works, was to become another global brand.

Bryant & May's 'Scottish Bluebell' has survived over a century. 'Three Torches' is Belgium's best-known brand, 'Allumettes de Sûreté' France's favourite.

An early version of Brazil's 'Beija-Flor' label pictured with Sweden's famous 'Swallow'.

First introduced in 1882,
South Africa's 'Lion'
brand.

Sweden's biggest-seller, the Solstickan charity label, with the label that was to become the best-known and most copied, Jönköpings' original 'Säkerhets Tändstickor'.

America's best-known brands:' Independence', 'Diamond' and 'Ohio', and Belgium's popular 'Camp' export label.

India's popular 'Horse Head' brand.

Holland's famous 'Windmill' label.

Germany's enduring 'Welt-Hölzer' label (above) has been updated since Heinrich Schmidt's original black-and-buff design.

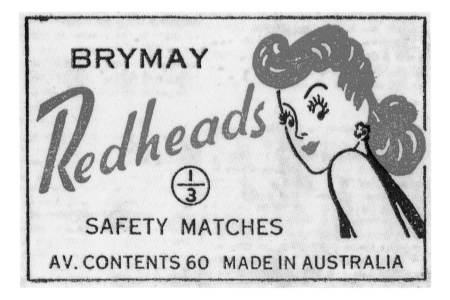

Varieties of Australia's successful 'Redheads' label.

H263

Redheads

CONTENTS 47 MATCHES

MADE IN AUSTRALIA. W.A. MATCH

H263

Redheads

CONTENTS 47 MATCHES

MADE IN AUSTRALIA. W.A. MATCH

Chapter Five

Image is Everything

In today's highly competitive consumer society, the release into the market of a product bearing no branding whatsoever would be considered economic suicide. Whatever the product, no matter how large or small, branding, be it in the form of an instantly recognisable symbol or a brand name, creates an identity. The customer connects with that identity and receives a perception of quality or value, which stimulates repeat sales.

Branding creates loyalty. Loyalty makes money.

So in the immensely competitive boom years that the match industry was enjoying at the end of the nineteenth century it was somewhat surprising to see a trend develop for labels printed only with patterns or pictures, and no manufacturers' name, no branding, nor any wording at all.

Perhaps manufacturers felt they had already made their mark. There was certainly no longer any need for lengthy and cumbersome instructions on how to strike matches, nor for elaborate manufacturer's claims about quality and performance. Pictures of their own factories, which all seemed uniformly dreary, also did little to fire

customers' imaginations. A combination of these elements was making for wordy and unattractive labels, and it was probably a recognition of this by match makers and a public desire for more attractive products that saw the beginning of a new stage in the development of matchbox labels – the decorative box.

The late nineteenth century was a time of great creativity in label design, and a source of much valuable and colourful material for collectors, although it was to be relatively shortlived.

In some examples, particularly from China and Japan, labels carried a simple, traditional pattern. A few labels of this kind were also briefly produced in Belgium (then Flanders). But in other parts of Europe, a wide range of high quality, brightly coloured and often glazed labels began to be produced, notably from factories in Sweden and Austria. The thin veneer of varnish on the labels provided an element of protection and gave them an attractive shine.

The subject matter was varied, but always pictorial: national costumes, folklore, famous faces, even romance and glamour, often in short sets for people to collect.

Colourful, glazed pictorial labels became the vogue at the start of the 20th century, like these from Austria (left), and Sweden (above).

Brightly coloured and of high quality, these boxes were definitely bought for their decorative value as well as for their contents, particularly in Europe where many of the themes were titillating and entertaining. Costume and fashion and pictures of glamorous lady socialites were in abundance, as was a certain amount of romantic symbolism.

The symbolism became much more apparent, however, in some of the labels produced in Sweden, Germany and Austria for export to lesser-developed markets such as Africa and Asia. Many of these brandless labels had what were perceived to be comical themes, with sometimes exotic foreign or ethnic images which would today be considered to be in questionable taste. But in those markets where literacy was low and communications poor, the image was more potent than the printed word. This aspect of marketing was to become of significant importance in later years with the growth of consumerism – and not just for the match industry.

Among some turn-of-the-century gems from Sweden were those depicting children's games, circus themes, humour and folklore. The ever-creative Jönköping factory produced some delightful sets of regional costumes and nymphs, none of which gave any clue to source or manufacturer. Their famous Pigmy series, however, subtly combined pictures of their most popular brand of matchbox being used by cherubs and imps as props for their mischievous antics.

The Swedish Uddevalla factory was another to turn out a number of highly symbolic pictorial labels, many for export to West Africa, with topics touching on literal and figurative black humour, the circus and children's games. Many of these, produced between 1893 and 1905, were supplied to Hamburg distributor Alfred Geisendörfer for export to the then German colony of Togoland and were sometimes used as the 'bottom' label for other company's brands.

Fashion and glamour were very popular themes in southern Europe

40

and South America at the start of the twentieth century. The Belgian firm of Roche et Cie. was extremely successful in distributing its attractive boxes of wax matches to these markets; adorned with softly-coloured photos of contemporary lady socialites and minor royalty, some of these boxes were exported to Cuba, as well as to France, Italy and Spain. One small firm in Paris used black and white pin-up pictures by famous photographer of the time, Felix Nadar, while a printer in Barcelona virtually monopolised trade in a new match-related item: the insert.

Like cigarette cards, inserts were placed inside the little Spanish matchboxes, and for some twenty years were extremely popular. Produced in sets of 75, they invariably featured royalty, socialites, actresses, bullfighters or other figures of note. They were distributed in South America and some European countries, as well as Spain, before disappearing in about 1910.

This brief and colourful phase in the development of the matchbox label was important. It showed manufacturers the value of attractive presentation, and exposed a need to communicate commercially in widely diverse markets. Of course, not all matchboxes were brandless at this time – far from it. But the need for recognition of these brands was confirmed, as was the importance of visual impact.

Opposite page: some of Jönköpings' famous Pigmy series. Above: costumes from the same company and below, side panels from Roche vesta boxes.

VIERLÄNDERIN.

GUDBRANDSDALEN.

RÄTTVIK (DALARNA)

SVENSKA TÄNDSTICKS AKTIEBOLAGET, SWEDEN

ÄLVDAL (VÄRMLAND)

SVENSKA TÄNDSTICKS AKTIEBOLAGET, SWEDEN

WINGÅKER

SVENSKA TÄNDSTICKS AKTIEBOLAGET, SWEDEN

VÄREND (SMÅLAND)

SVENSKA TÄNDSTICKS AKTIEBOLAGET, SWEDEN

Costumes and fairies from Sweden.

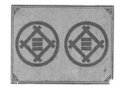

Humorous themes on these early export labels from Sweden and Austria. Some had simpler designs, like those from China and Flanders (bottom right).

S.ᴿᵀᴬ MARIA TERESA GARCIA

S.ᴿᵀᴬ MARIA RUIZ

S.ᴿᵀᴬ AURELIA HERRERA

S.ᴿᵀᴬ LUCRECIA VIVES

Glamorous ladies of the day featured on these wax vesta boxes by the Belgian firm of Roche et Cie. (top). The black-and-white pinup by Felix Nadar on an early French box contrasts with the glazed Austrian labels on either side.

MADE IN AUSTRIA

SWEET MAIDENHOOD

CLICHÉ NADAR PARIS

DANCING LADY

MADE IN AUSTRIA

Typical Swedish export label, issued between 1893-1905.

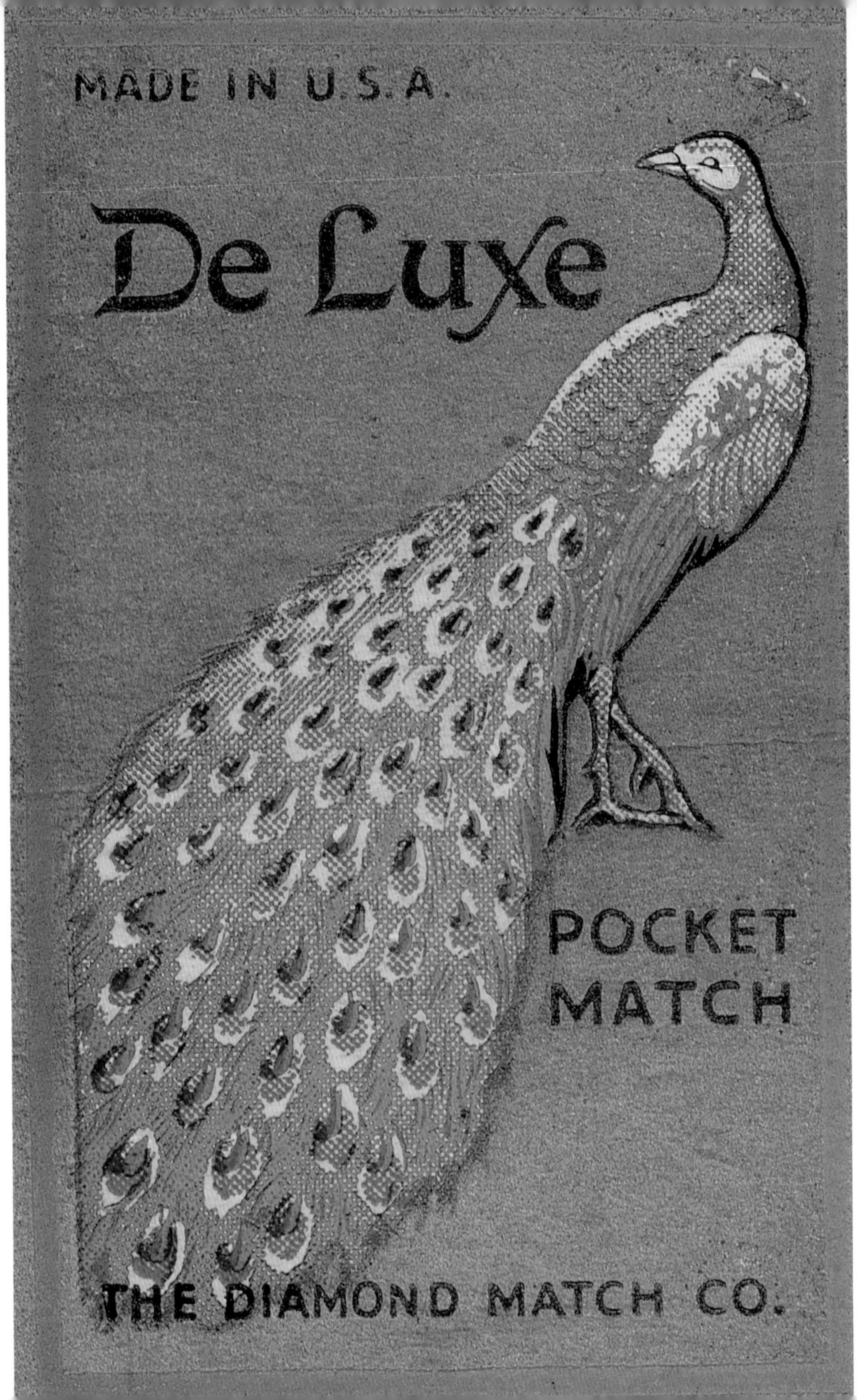
MADE IN U.S.A.
De Luxe
POCKET
MATCH
THE DIAMOND MATCH CO.

Chapter Six

Striking Success

The match industry was about to enter its golden age. The years leading up to the first world war saw a phenomenal global demand for the new wonder product, the safety match. In industrialised European and western nations as well as in the United States there was a seemingly insatiable need for matches, partly attributable to a simultaneous increase in the popularity of smoking. Domestic and household demand in these countries, a well as in the developing markets of Asia, Africa and elsewhere in the Americas was to focus the minds of manufacturers very sharply on their distribution and marketing skills, and the manufacturing challenges of producing matches that would work in humid tropical climates were having to be met.

Competition was becoming intense as the big names wrestled for markets and increasingly encountered the offloading of poor quality products from the multitude of small companies springing up around the world, cottage industries, counterfeiters and the like.

The brand was once again to become all-important, and just as John Walker found out after he first sold his label-less matches the new manufacturers were soon to discover, in the face of fierce competition, the need for clear identity and immediate recognition.

Not surprisingly, European manufacturers found it hard to meet demand during the first world war. Obtaining supplies of the necessary chemicals became almost impossible, and shipping and distribution were severely hit. Meeting domestic needs became a priority. Exports suffered, foreign manufacturers gained ground.

Production and sales saw a healthy and rapid revival between the wars, and while the match industry suffered badly again in world war two it had become more globally diversified and had more widespread resources. But history was to show that the match industry had probably already reached the peak of its success in the first part of the twentieth century – a time when the matchbox label was to proliferate in countless varieties.

Peacocks from Diamond Match Co. (USA) and Nitedals of Norway.

SUÉDE
Tändsticksfabriks Aktiebolaget
Phoenix i Malmö
MADE IN
utan svafvel
PARAFFINERADE
SWEDEN
och fosfor
SÄKERHETS TÄNDSTICKOR
TÄNDA ENDAST MOT LÅDANS PLÅN
SVERIGE
SCHWEDEN
SWEDEN

Præmiebelönnet paa Verdensudstillingen
i PARIS 1878
REGISTERED
N.º 008
TRADE MARK
1880
H.E. GOSCH & Cᵒˢ TÆNDSTIKFABRIKER
KJØBENHAVN.

Vulcans Tändsticksfabriks Patent
TRADE MARK
MADE IN
SWEDEN
utan svafvel
IMPREGNERADE
och fosfor
SÄKERHETS-TÄNDSTICKOR

Vulcans Tändsticksfabriks Patent
TRADE MARK
MADE IN
SWEDEN
utan svafvel
IMPREGNERADE
och fosfor
SÄKERHETS-TÄNDSTICKOR

Top right:
The phoenix rises from the
ashes on this early Danish
box (1880) and on others
from Sweden and South
Africa.

S.A. MATCH CO.(PTY)LTD.
SAFETY
PHOENIX
MATCH
VEILIGHEIDS
VUURHOUTJIES
S.A. Match Co (Pty) Ltd.

A parrot from the USA, an eagle from South Africa. The modern Italian version of the Swedish Three Stars brand ('Tre Stelle') was made in Spain for Swedish Match and carries the Italian tax stamp identifying them as Svedesi – Swedish quality.

Chapter Seven

Quality, Please

Customers wanted matches that would strike first time and burn evenly, and which wouldn't snap or smell.

In Britain they might have asked for Bryant & May's by name, in Sweden Jönköpings. In other places they might have particularly asked for Swedish matches (in Italy today ordinary matches are still described as 'Svedesi' to identify them apart from the popular wax 'cerini'), while an American tobacco store customer might have requested Diamond brand. In Africa and Asia the import of foreign matches was to grow as fast as local production. There was a considerable difference in quality, and when buying matches the customer was likely to say 'no, not those, I want the ones with the lion on'. So a readily recognisable label, probably with a locally-relevant theme, was to become a key selling factor.

Animals proved to be by far the richest source of label themes, and while they often appeared in varying degrees of anatomical accuracy they provided exotic images for Europeans, and familiar ones elsewhere.

The lion is still a dominant brand in South Africa, as it has been since 1905. Lions also featured prominently on the Lion Match Company's products in Malawi, Zimbabwe (then Southern Rhodesia), and Mozambique, and Bryant & May first launched a Lion brand in 1900. There was no shortage of lion themes in Sweden, where factories in Örebro, Tidaholm, Wexiö, Westervik, Uddevalla, Nybro, Nassjö, and Lidköping, among others, all used the king of the jungle to identify their wares in local and foreign markets. At least forty Indian factories used the lion as their logo, with Japan offering another dozen or so, both countries indulging in varying degrees of plagiarism and downright faking.

Tigers from India (opposite), and Hungary (above).

*Lions from Palestine,
Italy and Japan.*

Italy offered several lion labels, some of which were exported to Ethiopia, and the former Nur match factory in Acre, Palestine, featured a lion trademark, later duplicated by the El Bark factory in Damour, Lebanon.

Zanzibar, Macau, USA, Malaysia, Holland, Portugal, Ivory Coast and Morocco too all favoured lions.

Bryant & May's Tiger brand first bared its teeth in 1876 and survived over 100 years. The tiger was also a popular illustration for labels from Portugal, Italy, Burma, Hungary and India, among others.

Over the years India was to produce a huge variety of animal labels, ranging from snakes to sharks, frogs to dogs, as well as squirrels, kangaroos, monkeys, rabbits, zebra, crocodiles, cows, camels, rhino, bulls and bears, foxes, goats, bison, oxen, ostriches and elephants. The best-known is probably the Western India Match Co. (WIMCO) brand, The Horses' Head.

Sweden's label output was equally diverse, even in the late nineteenth century. Among wildlife themes favoured by some of the smaller factories were elks, donkeys, squirrels, crabs, parakeets, ostriches, bees, peacocks and dragons. Many of these were copied and elaborated on by the Japanese, who favoured monkeys, rabbits, bats and elephants.

Elephants too were highly popular emblems, especially in Africa and Asia where they were instantly recognisable as symbols of strength and reliability. Bryant & May issued an elephant label in 1876, as did Sweden's Jönköping factory. Later, companies in Italy, Belgium, Ceylon

(Sri Lanka), Norway, Nigeria and Sierra Leone followed suit. Portugal's Cia. Lusitana de Fósforos issued theirs in 1928, one of a number of animal-themed export labels from this factory, and Elephant Brand is almost certainly Thailand's best known.

With Sweden still a dominant producer their labels spread far and wide, adapted for local or foreign consumption. Apart from themes already mentioned, the Alsings factory issued the attractive Salamander brand in 1890, while Jönköping produced a chameleon, Uddevalla a rat and Lidköping a bulldog and a horse.

The Norwegian company Nitedals used the Running Horse to symbolise their long-lived 'protection from fire' slogan, originally issued in 1872. They also issued an attractive giraffe label. The camel was popularised by Portugal, Belgium and Egypt, the zebra by Portuguese, Belgian and Italian companies. The llama, naturally enough, was the people's favourite in Peru, while the fox found favour in Belgium and Britain, which also produced a Wild Boar brand.

The rhino graced labels in Sweden, Nepal, Hong Kong and Japan, and the crocodile was used in Italy. Sudan's Modern Match Company used the crocodile ('tumsah' in Arabic) as their main brand in later years (1965-74), no doubt inspired by the

many members of the species that inhabited the River Nile, not far from their factory.

Many emerging African nations in more modern history were to choose indigenous animals as trade marks for a variety of domestic products, not only matches. Zambian match-boxes had a buffalo on them, Malawi a leopard, Kenya's East African Match Co. a giraffe. South Africa's Nelson Match Company was to be long survived by the Springbok brand which it issued in 1909, the theme being carried on by the Lion Match Co. who also issued Impala and Blesbok brands.

The seemingly inexhaustible sets of labels issued by companies all over the world in the 1950s and 1960s to help combat declining sales followed many of the main themes chosen by factories in the early years, particularly animals.

A cat and a lion from India, the original Lion label from Sweden, and a later adaptation from Rhodesia.

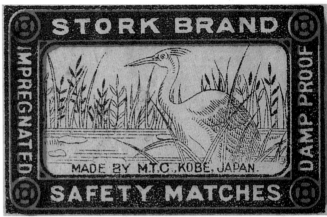

Early Japanese labels often depicted storks or cranes and were well drawn, unlike the Indian 'Luck Duck'. The condor was popular in South American markets.

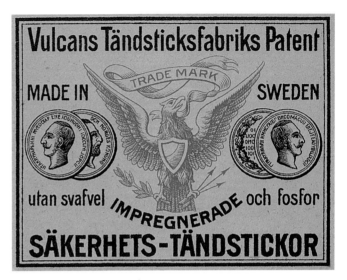

Swedish 'Condor' brand,
Vulcans Phoenix and
an American Eagle.

This label featuring Australia's national bird was first registered in Sweden in 1898.

Birds were also highly popular label themes, perhaps demonstrated by the fact that they represent some of the oldest existing brands. Sweden's ubiquitous Swallow first appeared in the late 1890s and is still available, like Bryant & May's Swan Vestas, first introduced in 1883.

Swift, another Bryant & May brand, was also a strong survivor, although not originally introduced until the 1920s by Maguire & Paterson, the Dublin-based match maker in which Bryant & May held an interest before ultimately acquiring the company in 1981. Sweden's Uddevalla factory, which launched the Swallow, was to introduce another highly successful brand in 1894 with its colourful Condor label, a theme pursued in Portugal, Bolivia and Ecuador. Four years later, the same factory – one of the most prolific of its time – put its Kookaburra brand onto the market. It was to remain popular for many years, notably in Australia.

The humming bird (Beija-Flor) was to be the brand for Brazilians – among the world's largest consumers of matches – and the parrot was popular too. In Japan, where labels of the late 1800s and early 1900s were either intricate miniature works of art or extremely crude, cranes and storks were frequently depicted.

The eagle, however, was probably the most frequently found flying creature on the world's matchboxes and appeared in many countries including Great Britain, USA, Burma, Hong Kong, Costa Rica, Belgium, and, from 1936, on labels of the National Match Co. of South Africa.

An attractive Belgian cockatoo label was matched by an owl from Italy and an ostrich from Denmark; that country's Hellerup & Glødefrij offered a fine falcon, while the toucan was used from Portugal to British Guiana. The peacock was popular in Burma, and Nitedals of Norway also produced a fine example. In later years, the American Diamond Match Co. produced an attractive number of labels featuring brightly coloured exotic birds. AMC of Uganda used the crane, and in Mauritius the New Light Match Co. naturally enough used the island's national emblem – the dodo – as its trademark.

While Hong Kong offered the dove and Holland the penguin, India maintained its seemingly endless output of creatures of all kinds, not always immediately recognisable.

Finally, the mythological Phoenix has to get a mention. Symbolically rising from the ashes, as did so many of the early match producers, the phoenix was to be a popular brand for the Swedish Vulcan match factory who used it from 1879, although a phoenix label had been issued in Malmö in 1874. H.E.Gosch & Co. of Denmark issued their own Phoenix in 1880, and another appeared in South

Africa in 1899 issued by the factory of the same name, to be revived later by the South African Match Co.

The natural world was a source of inspiration for many other designs, trees, fish, flowers and insects included.

Again, Sweden's factories provided many attractive early varieties, including Rose, Lily, and Three Tulips brands from Södertelje, Neck Rose from Lidköping (1898), and Butterfly brand from Tidaholm, issued in about 1908. Another delicately-drawn butterfly was produced in Flanders, and in later years was to become a popular brand in Holland under its local name, Vlinder. Holland was also to produce Cactus and Dolphin brands, and popular Belgian brands were Camellia, Flanders Charm (a poppy), and later, Violet. The Japanese favoured cherry trees, carnations, chrysanthemums and goldfish. Australia also issued a Carnation brand, and Finland an Iris.

Some of the best known and most enduring brands were labels depicting their country of origin's national flower, like the Lion Match Co. of South Africa's Protea, first issued in 1922, and Edelweiss from the Solo Match Works of Austria.

Pacific Manufacturers of Fiji supply the island with locally-made Hibiscus brand matches, while Sweden's Palm Tree brand is still available in African export markets after nearly a century.

All of these labels, with their colourful and sometimes bizarre interpretations, represent just the beginning of the battle for the brands.

Butterflies on labels from Sweden and Holland, and a Dutch penguin.

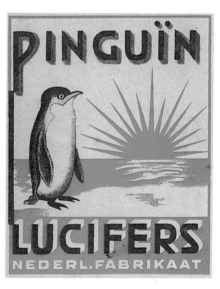

*Duncan's 'Carnation'
brand from Australia,
and 'Violet' from
Belgium (1926).*

Colourful and attractive, plants and flowers were popular label themes for manufacturers world-wide, like these from Belgium, Sweden, Austria, South Africa and Holland.

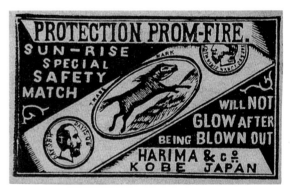

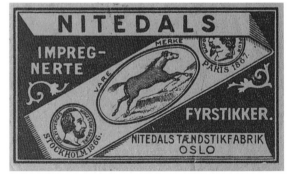

An ostrich dominates this Danish label, while the 'Running Horse' has symbolised Nitedals of Norway since 1872. Spot the Japanese fake in the middle.

Opposite page: From ants to bears, no creature was too humble or huge to go on a Swedish matchbox label. The Sudanese 'Tumsah' (crocodile) brand was produced from 1965; the Italian version is earlier.

Marine life from India (shark, crab), and Holland, (dolphin).

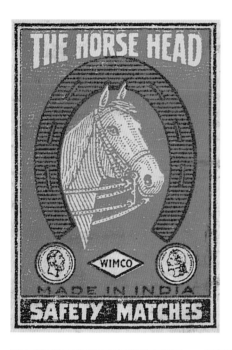

THE HORSE HEAD

WIMCO

MADE IN INDIA

SAFETY MATCHES

THE ZEBRA

IMPREGNATED
SAFETY MATCHES

TRADE MARK   MADE IN ITALY

HORSE BRAND

MAHBUBIA MATCH CO., MAHBUBABAD.

THREE MONKEYS

WIMCO

SAFETY MATCHES
MADE IN INDIA

COW HEAD

SHUNMUGA MATCH FACTORY PERUNDURAI

SAFETY MATCHES

IMPREG-   NATED
GIRAFFE
LICENSED   MATCH
SAFETY   MATCH
MADE BY NITEDALS NORWAY.

Animals were popular themes for Indian labels such as Horse Head, Cow Head, Horse and Three Monkeys. Zebra (Italy) and Giraffe (Norway) were popular export brands.

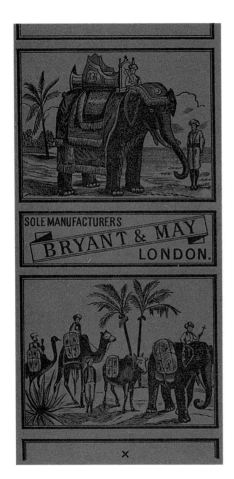

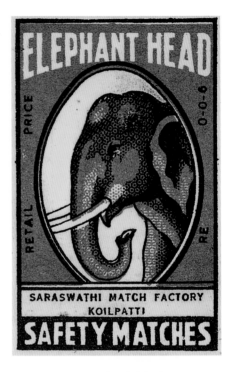

*Bryant & May's
Elephant didn't last as
long as it's Thai counter-
part, probably that
country's best-known
label. Elephants were
popular in India and on
Swedish export labels for
the far east.*

South Africa's national animal, the springbok, features on old (vertical, 1935) and more recent (horizontal, 1971) labels from the Lion Match Co., along with Impala (1939). 'Palm Tree' and 'Stag' are yet more Swedish varieties.

Chapter Eight

Trains, Boats & Flying Machines

The development of the safety match in the early nineteenth century came about at a time of great global industrialisation. It was a time of pioneering engineering, grand buildings, iron steamships and the rapid development of locomotives, motor cars and aircraft.

Highly topical and ever changing, these subjects also provided much inspiration for matchbox label design, particularly transportation. New, more efficient ships and railroads were changing – and diminishing – the world.

Smoke and fire were evidently close to the hearts of early matchmakers, who produced numerous steam engine designs. Leading among them, as ever, were the Swedes. In 1904 Jönköping registered a very simple 'Engine' design, but it was Anneberg's 'Locomotiv', which appeared in several different varieties and colours and in both vertical and horizontal formats, which was probably the best-known label of this type. The Sirius factory produced the attractive and colourful 'Express' brand in about 1910 showing an early train steaming along a lakeside at the foot of a mountain.

In 1888, the very small partnership of Ginsberg & Toennessen of King William's Town, South Africa, produced their first and possibly only brand, Locomobile. This rare and attractive example appeared to depict what we would today call a traction engine, at work in a farmer's field. The brand was to last only a couple of years after the partnership split up.

Britain's North of England Match Company was to depict Stephenson's famous 'Rocket' engine some years later, and engines and trains of all kinds continued to be a popular subject for matchbox labels for many years.

Despite the importance of the role that railways were to play in India, that country was relatively slow to produce its own railway-related labels to start with, but was soon to catch up, issuing a huge variety of brands on the same theme. Among them were 'Silver Arrow', 'Golden Train', 'Express' and 'Engine'.

Early Austrian and Japanese companies, however, were quick to adopt the theme for their labels.

Transport of all kinds appears on matchbox labels. Opposite page: a Japanese monkey drives a carriage, while above this 1888 label for a South African manufacturer shows an early traction engine.

Man wrapped up
in hissen maks a
vary small parcel.

3794

'England's Glory' was first issued in 1891. Today the old brand is in a new box. 'England's Glory' –made in Sweden.

More familiar to most people in the developing world markets, and more integral to the transport of matches and their components, were ships. This was the time when the great sailing clippers were giving way to the awesome new steamships, and this was very much depicted on matchbox labels of the time. Best-known of all is probably Sweden's famous 'Ship' brand. First issued by the Södertelje factory as just 'Ship' brand, it was later acquired by Jönköping-Vulcan and became 'The Ship'. The label, which first appeared in about 1882, quickly became familiar and popular in Sweden and in many export markets, including Britain. It remained in circulation for almost a hundred years and was to be much copied.

Sweden issued a variety of early 'Steamer' brands, while the most famous to come out of Britain was certainly S & J Morelands' 'England's Glory', first issued in 1891, later to become a Bryant & May brand, and still available.

Another early label, one of many colourful glazed labels to be issued by the B.Fürth Company of Vienna, showed the paddlewheeler 'Briliant' (sic) in full steam.

In the USA, the Barber Match Co. of St. Louis, Missouri and Akron, Ohio, issued cardboard boxes of 'Steamboat' matches in 1881, illustrated with a twin-funnelled paddle steamer. In 1918 the Diamond Match Co. was selling its 'Ocean Liner' safety matches in America, a similar label being used by Canada's Eddy Match Co. Some years later the National Safety Match Corp. issued its 'Big River' brand in the USA, with a picture of a paddle steamer called Mayflower on its label. Diamond Match reverted to sail with its 'American Clipper' brand.

Japanese manufacturers seemed to be fond of nautical themes at the turn of the century. The Shinagawa Company of Osaka produced a blatant copy of the Swedish 'Ship' label, and a variety of paddle steamers and sailing ship brands were available. The Nippon Matchmanufacturnig Co.Ltd. (sic) issued a label showing a pair of twin-funnelled ironclads. Several brands of the time, variously called 'Ship', 'Steamer', and 'Lifeboat'

*Cycles and carriages from
Sweden and Belgium.*

Balloons from Holland and Sweden.

all shared the same image: a large steamship with two funnels, while another showed a three-funnelled steamer and a primitive biplane on course to collide with each other or a fast-approaching iceberg.

By way of a change, Universe brand, issued in Belgium in the 1880s and by the Swedish Hvetlanda factory, showed an early steam-powered submarine.

Another great innovation of the era was the motor car, which was to appear in countless varieties on match-box labels around the world. By the late nineteenth century motoring was becoming an extremely fashionable pastime, and matchmakers even produced special windproof matches for motorists. Bryant & May's 'Motor Match' brand, sold in slim card boxes or tins, were said to be 'for motor cars, launches, yachts & c. Will flame for 20 seconds and keep alight in the strongest wind'. R.Bell & Co., a company eventually bought by Bryant & May, produced 'Wind Vestas, for use on motors, cycles and yachts'.

One of the earliest illustrations of a motor car appeared in the 1880s on Jönköpings' Automobil label, which shows what looks like a three-wheeled Benz. The Wexiö factory of Sweden issued its own Motor Car brand, but the most popular was probably The Automobile brand, issued by the nearby Kalmar Mönsterås factory.

The Automobile appeared in a variety of colours and designs, the style of the car being updated as the years went by. In 1912 the Swedish Hvetlanda factory produced a bizarre 'Flying Motor Car' design for export to India, presumably to capitalize on the other great passion of the time: flying.

Flying machines of all kinds were soon to be commonplace on match-box labels, including hot air balloons. A charming early balloon label from Japan shows a rather overdressed couple enjoying a balloon flight. She is tightly grasping the edge of the steeply-tilting basket, while he casually plays a mandolin. A balloon is also the emblem chosen for Jönköpings Appollo label, issued in about 1881, while the Toyo Match Co. of Kobe, Japan, chose an 'Airship'.

A Russian label of the time shows a primitive biplane, to reappear later as the 'Avion' export brand, while Jönköping too showed an early biplane on their 1908 'Aeroplane' brand.

A brand imported to Britain by J.John Masters & Co. in the same year, also called 'Aeroplane', used a flimsy monoplane design.

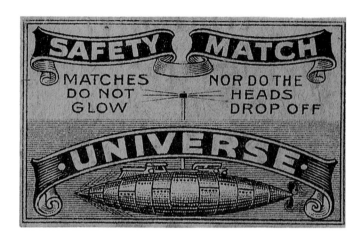

SAFETY MATCH

MATCHES DO NOT GLOW — NOR DO THE HEADS DROP OFF

·UNIVERSE·

Impregnated

CHAR-A-BANC
SAFETY MATCHES

Made in Finland

Impregnated

THE CLIFTON SUSPENSION BRIDGE "SAFETY

MADE IN HOLLAND

SAFETY MATCH

THE PALKI

SAFETY MATCH

MADE IN AUSTRIA

BRYANT AND MAY'S
MOTOR MATCH
FOR MOTOR CARS, LAUNCHES, YACHTS &c
WILL FLAME FOR 20 SECONDS AND KEEP ALIGHT IN THE STRONGEST WIND

Transport and technology were dominant themes as the 20th century dawned, with no limit to creativity. Subjects ranged from the steam-powered submarine on this Belgian 'Universe' label to the char-a-banc and dramatic new Clifton suspension bridge. The giant sedan chair on the Austrian 'Palki' label was slightly behind the times. As the car developed, Bryant & May introduced its 'Motor Matches'.

But meanwhile, at the start of the twentieth century, the use of matches was becoming more and more widespread thanks to better distribution and an increase in smoking and so the themes on their labels became more diverse.

Every imaginable mode of transport was eventually to appear on matchbox labels. The popular Finnish 'Char-a-Banc' brand showing a primitive open-topped bus must have seemed positively modern compared to the selection of canoes, catamarans, gondolas and rafts, bicycles, tricycles, tandems and penny-farthings, buses, trolleybuses and trams, oxcarts, ostrich carts, carriages and sedan chairs, skis and skates shown on competitors' labels of the time.

Even revolutionary new feats of engineering were represented in this, the great leap forward of industriali-sation, including the Clifton Suspension Bridge which was to appear on a Wexiö factory export label in Britain in 1893, and on a similar label made in Holland the following year.

The explosive growth of railways, cars and aircraft, which still continues to accelerate, has remained a topical theme in matchbox label design over the years, and transport has always been a popular theme for manufacturers and distributors to use as the content for collectors' sets as a way to arrest the dramatic decline in match sales during the 1950s and 1960s.

Early flying machines on labels from USSR and Sweden.

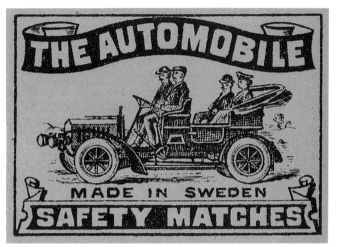

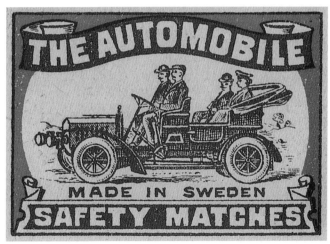

The age of motoring provided exciting new subject matter for match makers, as these Swedish examples show.

Railway engines fired the imagination for many, and soon found their way onto matchboxes.

The age of steam was changing. The charming and colourful 'Express' label from 1910 idealises rail travel, while the combination of steam and sail is pictured on this early Swedish label, and on a Japanese copy of the same period. The Austrian 'Trolley Car' was much more advanced.

Ferocious battleships – note the nautical frame – contrast with a peaceful fishing scene on these two old Japanese labels (top left and left). The top 'Ocean Liner' label was issued by Canada's Eddy Match Co., the lower one by America's Diamond Match Co. in 1918. The earlier paddlewheeler below is an attractive glazed label from B.Fürth of Vienna.

NIPPON MATCHMANUFACTURNIG CO.,LTD.

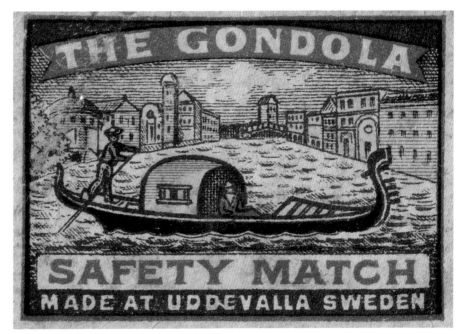

'Canoemen' shoot the rapids in this dramatic Swedish label (top left) while the Japanese and Indian labels (top) seem to depict impending naval disasters. The Swedish 'Gondola' is an altogether more peaceful image. The Barber Match Co. issued the rare 'Steamboat' matches in the USA in 1881. 'Big River' and 'Clipper' are later American brands.

MADE IN AUSTRIA

REGISTERED

H.M.Queen Alexandra

MADE IN AUSTRIA

REGISTERED

H.M.Queen Alexandra

MADE IN AUSTRIA

REGISTERED

H.M.Queen Alexandra

MADE IN AUSTRIA

REGISTERED

H.M.King Edward VII

MADE IN AUSTRIA

REGISTERED

H.M.King Edward VII

MADE IN AUSTRIA

REGISTERED

H.M.King Edward VII

Chapter Nine

Variety: The Spice of Sales

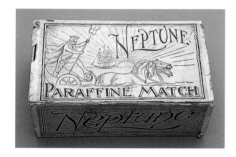

Royalty was an ever-popular matchbox label theme. This uncut sheet of glazed Austrian labels (left) features Queen Alexandra and King Edward VII. Above, Neptune appears on an unusual Diamond Match box from 1880.

The need to be different and easily identifiable was of course just one challenge that manufacturers constantly had to face, as was the expanding variety of ethnic tastes and cultures that their ever-growing markets presented.

Events, places, sport, professions and atmospheric and evocative local topics were exploited to their limits, as were people. Real people and imaginary people, people in folklore, religion and mythology.

Naturally enough, royalty – traditionally the people's favourite people – featured prominently on many a domestic matchbox. Members of royal families appeared not only on boxes in their home countries, particularly in Britain, Belgium, Denmark and the Netherlands, but in many others too. Although Sweden had a monarchy, the number of matchbox labels this giant among producers issued of its own royal family was relatively few. Gustav Vasa, Gustavus Adolfus, King Oscar II and King Eric XIV were far outnumbered by locally-issued labels commemorating foreign royalty or royal occasions.

British royalty appeared on labels from Austria, Czechoslovakia, Belgium and India among others, and, of course, on home-grown brands and those from Sweden. Sweden's Vulcan factory produced brands called 'England's Royal Pair' and 'Royal Matches', both labels depicting His Majesty King George V and Queen Mary, 'Emperor of India', and another showing the Duke and Duchess of Connaught. Queen Victoria was to feature on several Swedish labels, one celebrating her Diamond Jubilee in 1887. The Prince of Wales, who also made a brief appearance as Edward VIII, is also included in the gallery of brands issued by Swedish companies as did Queen Wilhelmina of the Netherlands and Henry VIII. Queen Wilhelmina appeared on several labels, particularly in the Netherlands, both as a young princess and at various stages of her reign, as did Queen Juliana.

Military leaders too were popularly used as trademarks during this era of imperialism and proliferating power struggles. Sweden's Vulcan factory issued 'Lord Kitchener of Kartoum' (sic) brand, while the Swedish Match Co. issued 'General Gordon'. 'Napoleon' brand appeared on another Swedish-produced matchbox just before the first world war,

*Schubert and Buffalo
Bill on labels from
Austria and USA.*

and the Wexiö factory issued a set of labels showing military men, including Major General Kitchener, Lieutenant General Lord Methuen, General Sir Redvers Butler and Major General Baden-Powell who, incidentally, was briefly a director of Swedish Match in London at the time. Austria issued 'The Heroes' brand, picturing Viscount Kitchener and Earl Roberts, in both glazed and unglazed versions.

The trend for matchbox labels to feature royal and military figures was to long outlast that of the Spanish matchbox inserts which frequently featured the same themes. But the variety of people depicted on matchbox labels was to become much greater.

Schubert appeared on an Austrian label, Buffalo Bill on an American one. The Danish company H.E.Gosch featured the explorer Tordenskjold on their early labels, where he still appears to this day, and other prominent figures to be immortalised on matchboxes at the time include Abraham Lincoln, Karl Marx, Paul Kruger, Nero, Garibaldi, Gandhi and many others. George Washington appeared on an early (1876) Collard, Kendall & Co. box, reissued in 1900 as a Bryant & May brand, and a Belgian label featuring first world war heroine nurse Edith Cavell was both popular and controversial at the time. While meant to commemorate her

bravery it was issued without her family's consent and caused considerable distress.

In subsequent years personalities and celebrities from all walks of life were to brand matchboxes, one of the first modern icons being Shirley Temple, who made her debut on a matchbox from Iran.

Figures from religion also provided powerful images, particularly in Asia. This theme was ruthlessly exploited by both local and European manufacturers, giving rise to a number of labels that ranged from intricately-engraved, delicately-coloured miniature masterpieces to crude, vulgar and sometimes offensive attempts to capture sales.

Austrian and Swedish factories published several lengthy and colourful glazed sets of labels for Indian and Asian consumption featuring holy or revered people, living and dead, as well a number of gods. India's own home market produced literally hundreds of varieties on the theme of gods and religious mythology, with Kali, Krishna, Vishnu, Hanuman, Ganesha and others portrayed in innumerable roles.

Japan's most popular deities included the seven gods of good fortune, beauty, courage, wisdom and longevity included. Most frequently pictured were Hotei, Ebisu, Bishaman and Fukuroka.

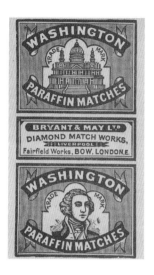

Washington appears as a place and a person in this 1895 design (top left). Earl Roberts is surrounded by different versions of the Danish 'Tordenskjold' brand, accompanied by Wellington (front and back panels), a young Queen Wilhelmina of the Netherlands, and Gandhi. At bottom right is the controversial 'Miss Cavell' label.

Japan also issued labels depicting Christ and the Madonna and child, both of which were considered highly offensive at the time and were withdrawn from European markets as inappropriate themes for commercial exploitation. Meanwhile, European manufacturers flooded Asia with their own brands, no doubt causing their own share of offence from time to time. Jönköpings 'Fakir' label may or may not have been one of these, while the British firm of R.Bell & Co., who issued 'Adam and Eve – the first match' in 1899 had nothing to be ashamed of.

The mild outrage caused by those Japanese labels depicting Christian images would be insignificant if some of the European brands aimed at ethnic and colonial markets were to be issued today. Large numbers of labels aimed at presenting evocative ethnic messages were destined for African and Asian colonies of France, Belgium, Italy and Britain. Some were attractive, artistic. Others were imperious, or meant to be funny. Brands such as Nigger, Jolly Nigger-boy, Coon, Blackamoor, Jap Girls and Gollywog were not uncommon, and were remarkably popular.

Many labels aimed at these markets had motifs of palm trees, wild animals, mud huts and 'natives' of various types, particularly bare-breasted women.

A number of labels combined glamour with exotic surroundings. The Swedish 'Abyssinian' of 1885 shows a shapely girl balancing a water pot on her head. 'Swinging Belle', 'Daisy', 'Goan Beauty' and 'Indian Actor' were all Swedish issues of the 1880s, followed by later issues such as Temptress (Sirius, 1910), a girl on a swing; The Hammock, (1914), a girl in a hammock; and La Hamaca, (The Swing), where another young lady enjoys what was evidently a popular pursuit of the time.

From the Alsings factory in 1890 came 'The Hindoo' (sic), showing the aforementioned gentleman with two bullocks pulling a cartload of matches. The Jinricksha brand (1886) shows a rather disoriented Chinese gentleman with a rickshaw, surrounded by palm trees. Other Swedish brands of the time were 'The Oriental' (1879), 'The Chinaman' (1885), 'Rajah' (Annebergs, 1889), 'The Sheikh' (Jönköping, 1906) and the 1914 Vulcan label 'The Chieftain' showing a fierce, sword-wielding native. 'Gavatya' is a well-drawn Wenersborgs label showing a well-dressed, turbanned gent playing a one-stringed fiddle.

The Austrian match industry had a big share of this type of branding and produced many pretty glazed sets of labels with diverse ethnic themes.

These included 'Indian Types' – a series of Indian ladies and Maharajahs – 'Sweet Maidenhood'; 'Dancing Lady' and 'The Fashion' – all sets. Some notable individual labels, out of many, include 'Lady with Fan', 'The Thakors Man', a turbanned man carrying a sabre and a large hunting horn, and 'The Palki', showing four turban-wearing bearers carrying a king-sized sedan chair.

The Solo Match Works of Czechoslovakia issued 'The Leaf Cutter', while a Dutch label from 1884 shows a spear-throwing, shield-wielding Zulu. Many more labels of European origin used native idols, masks, dolls, puppets or carvings at

Opposite page: Gods and saints and religious imagery were popular themes for export labels to Asia, like these showing the goddesses Kali (left) and Durga (right), and a fakir (centre).

Top: a number of labels produced in Japan depicting the Madonna and child and intended for European markets caused great offence and were quickly withdrawn. The Indian labels below celebrate Diwali – the festival of light – and the god Krishna.

A wide variety of ethnic
themes was exploited for
sale to developing markets
in Africa and Asia.

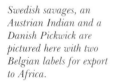

Swedish savages, an Austrian Indian and a Danish Pickwick are pictured here with two Belgian labels for export to Africa.

this time of ever-increasing diversity in matchbox label design.

From deities to royalty and tribal chieftains, beings of all kinds appeared on matchbox labels and characters from mythology, folklore and literature all turned out to be fair game.

A fine and rare example is a large box from the Diamond Match Co. of America, issued in about 1880, the 'Neptune Paraffine Match', which shows Neptune with his trident being borne into the sea in a chariot drawn by three horses. 'The Sorcerer' appeared on a Swedish label of 1886,

soon followed by Cupid, Hercules or Herkules and Mercury in various forms. Austria and Belgium both produced Centaur labels, Denmark 'Valkyrien'. India, China and Japan all maintained similar themes in their local production, depicting traditional culture and mythology.

Folklore and fairytale, legend and literature provided much more material for the seemingly inexhaustible needs of the match industry, still on the lookout for brands that would last. 'Little Boy Blue', first issued in 1888, was one such marque, appearing on boxes of matches exported from Sweden, Belgium and Finland in many varieties for many years. Another was 'Bo Peep', from Ireland's Maguire & Miller Co., (1904), later to become a Bryant & May subsidiary. 'William Tell' (1905) was another brand to survive many years, adorning labels from Finland, Austria, Czechoslovakia and Belgium. The British S & J Moreland company produced its famous 'John Bull' brand at the start of the twentieth century. Little Red Riding Hood popped up on British and Austrian labels, while Peter Pan was immortalised on Jönköping Vulcans' 1912 label. At about the same time a rotund Pickwick is personified on a Danish label, as is the adulterous Cossack Mazeppa on labels from the Swedish Wenersborg factory. Highwayman Dick Turpin came next, on another popular Belgian label (1913), with Tiny Tim (Finland), The Three Musketeers (Czechoslovakia) and Falstaff (Belgium) following soon after. King Cole was an Estonian import and 'Pandora and her Box' was a popular Russian label of the 1920s, roughly copied by the Japanese.

Connecting with people – reaching the end-user – was as important to match makers then as it is now for any product. Widening the range of subject matter even further, to include trades and professions, opened up a new avenue of exploitation for trade mark potential.

Perhaps the striking 'British Workman' brand of 1897 was the forerunner of these, but many more labels were subsequently to feature tradesmen and craftsmen in the following years. Perhaps the best-known was to be 'Pilot' (nautical, not airline), originally issued in 1899 by Maguire, Miller & Co. and ultimately to become a Bryant & May brand which stayed in production for almost a hundred years.

Of similar vintage, but with less staying power, were Drummer, Matador, Conjurer, Watchman and Beefeater , all Swedish labels first issued between 1884 and 1904. Other vintage labels of the time were 'Clown', from Holland, and 'Shepherd', from Norway. Belgium was to follow with 'Miners', and 'Butler' and 'Porter' brands were applied to labels from Czechoslovakia in the early 1920s. In the mid 20s the Judge brand could be seen on matches from Italy and Finland – one of the more enduring images – and a later label from America's Capitol Safety Match Corp. showed a gold prospector.

These were just a few of the activities depicted on matchboxes of the time, some of which were to vanish along with the pastimes they pictured. Longer-lasting, in reality if not in terms of sales, were famous landmarks and places, all of which have appeared on matchboxes at some time or another.

Like the Clifton Suspension Bridge mentioned earlier, London's Tower Bridge was to feature on several different labels over the years, first appearing in about 1899 on a Swedish label, later on one from Belgium. The Norwegians favoured London Bridge, while probably the most inspiring engineering achievement of its time, the Eiffel Tower, was also to appear as a match brand, the most attractive probably being the Swedish version of 1907.

Cleopatra's Needle, now on the Embankment in London, was pictured in situ in Egypt on a Bryant & May label of 1878, the year it was erected. The Pyramids were also to prove highly popular subject matter for matchbox labels, appearing in many varieties from around the world including, of course, Egypt.

While it is hardly surprising that monuments such as the Taj Mahal, the Red Fort or the Rock Fort should appear on Indian labels, some other subjects were much more esoteric. The Rock brand , depicting an outline of the outcrop which is Gibraltar, was used on exports from Finland, Holland and Flanders from about 1903. Austria issued 'Commonwealth Safety Matches',

WILLIAM TELL

MADE IN BELGIUM

AVERAGE 50 MATCHES

Finest Impregnated
Safety Matches

IMPREGNATED
SAFETY MATCHES

OM'S FAIRY TALE SERIES

MADE IN AUSTRIA

LITTLE RED RIDING HOOD
AVERAGE CONTENTS
50 STICKS

VALKYRIEN

DANSK FABRIKAT

Bo-Peep
SAFETY

Match
MADE IN BELFAST BY
MAGUIRE & PATERSON
(BELFAST) LT.P

IMPREGNATED
SAFETY MATCHES

LITTLE BOY BLUE
BRAND
MADE IN BELGIUM
AVERAGE CONTENTS 50 MATCHES

AVERAGE 50 MATCHES

KING COLE

IMPREGNATED
SAFETY
MATCHES

MADE IN ESTHONIA

*Characters from folklore
and fairytale, legend and
literature, all have decorated matchboxes over the
past century.*

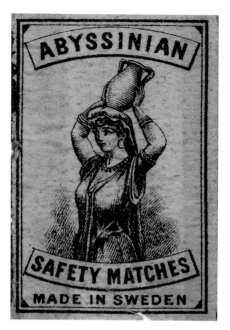

in numerous forms ranging through 'Velocipide', 'Hobby Horse' and 'Tricycle' brands. The Norwegian company of Bryn & Halden issued a 'Sport' brand in 1913 showing a gentleman apparently racing a penny-farthing.

with an outline map of Australia, and another with a map of the British Isles, while Belgium produced one of the United States. Belgium also produced 'Vesuvius' brand, and Holland an attractive rendition of the Palace of Peace in the Hague, issued from about 1908.

Disasters, achievements, victory, independence, coronations and jubilees, all proved irresistible to match makers and public alike. The Irish firm of Paterson & Co. showed St.Patrick ridding the island of snakes on their 'Ireland's Leading Light' brand of 1902. But above all it was royal occasions that were celebrated and sold, and there was plenty of

choice at this stage of the evolution of European royalty.

The Swedish Nybro factory produced a double header with its 'Imperial Topical Match' which jointly celebrated Queen Victoria's Diamond Jubilee of 1887 and the Silver Wedding of the Prince and Princess of Wales the following year, while the coronation of Queen Mary and King George was another popular theme.

As a final example of variety in early label design, another topical growth area was sport, and it too was frequently used in trade marks of the time.

Cycling was making an impact as a 'modern' pastime, and was depicted

Mostly issued between 1885-1914, colourful and exotic labels like these and those opposite were very popular in export markets.

H.R.H. THE PRINCE OF WALES — H.R.H. THE PRINCESS OF WALES

ICH DIEN

MADE IN AUSTRIA.

MADE IN AUSTRIA

BELGIUMS ROYAL COUPLE

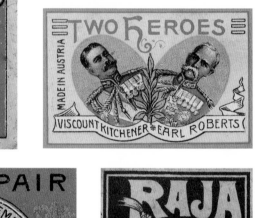

TWO HEROES

MADE IN AUSTRIA

VISCOUNT KITCHENER ✱ EARL ROBERTS

God save — King Edward VII. and Queen Alexandra

MADE IN AUSTRIA.

THE VICEREGAL PAIR

LORD CURZON — LADY CURZON

MADE IN AUSTRIA

ITALY'S ROYAL PAIR

QUEEN HELENA OF ITALY. — KING VITTORIO EMANUELE II.

MADE IN AUSTRIA

RAJA

SAFETY MATCHES
MADE IN FLANDERS

Royalty and military heroes were fre-
quently celebrated on high quality
labels like these, which commemorated
royal occasions or great victories.

Trades and professions were also well represented, with a wide variety of occupations used as label subjects.

Famous places and monuments increasingly appeared on matchbox labels as travel made them more familiar. Bryant & May's 'Cleopatra's Needle' was issued to celebrate its relocation to London's Embankment in 1878. A Swedish label represents the Sphinx in Gizeh, an Indian label the Red Fort.

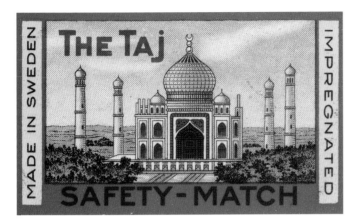

The Taj Mahal features on labels from Sweden and India (far left), the Palace of Peace in the Hague on a Dutch label from 1918. Bridges too were popular subject matter.

Sporting themes are shown here on an early Swedish example from about 1887 and, opposite: others from the Côte d'Ivoire and USA. The 'Sport' panel is part of a label from the Norwegian firm of Bryn & Halden, issued in 1913.

More demure was ice skating, as illustrated by the Belgian 'Skating Girl' label and Vulcan Globe's 'Ringking' which showed a skating couple.

Britain's Bryant & May issued a colourful 'Football Match' label in 1884, which actually seems to depict a rugby match, while Collard & Co. issued their 'Cricket Match'. 'The Tennis' was another British label of 1900, 'Trotting' a Swedish equestrian brand.

Jockeys, boxers, footballers, all made appearances on labels, as did indoor sports like card games and dominoes. America was later to celebrate its national sports with brands like 'Big League' from the National Safety Match Corp. showing a baseball game, and 'All American' (a football player) by Capitol Safety Match Corp.

These were just a few of the main subjects chosen by match companies in the years leading up to and into the twentieth century, and there were to be many, many more.

It was to be both a beginning, and an end, of an important era in match label design.

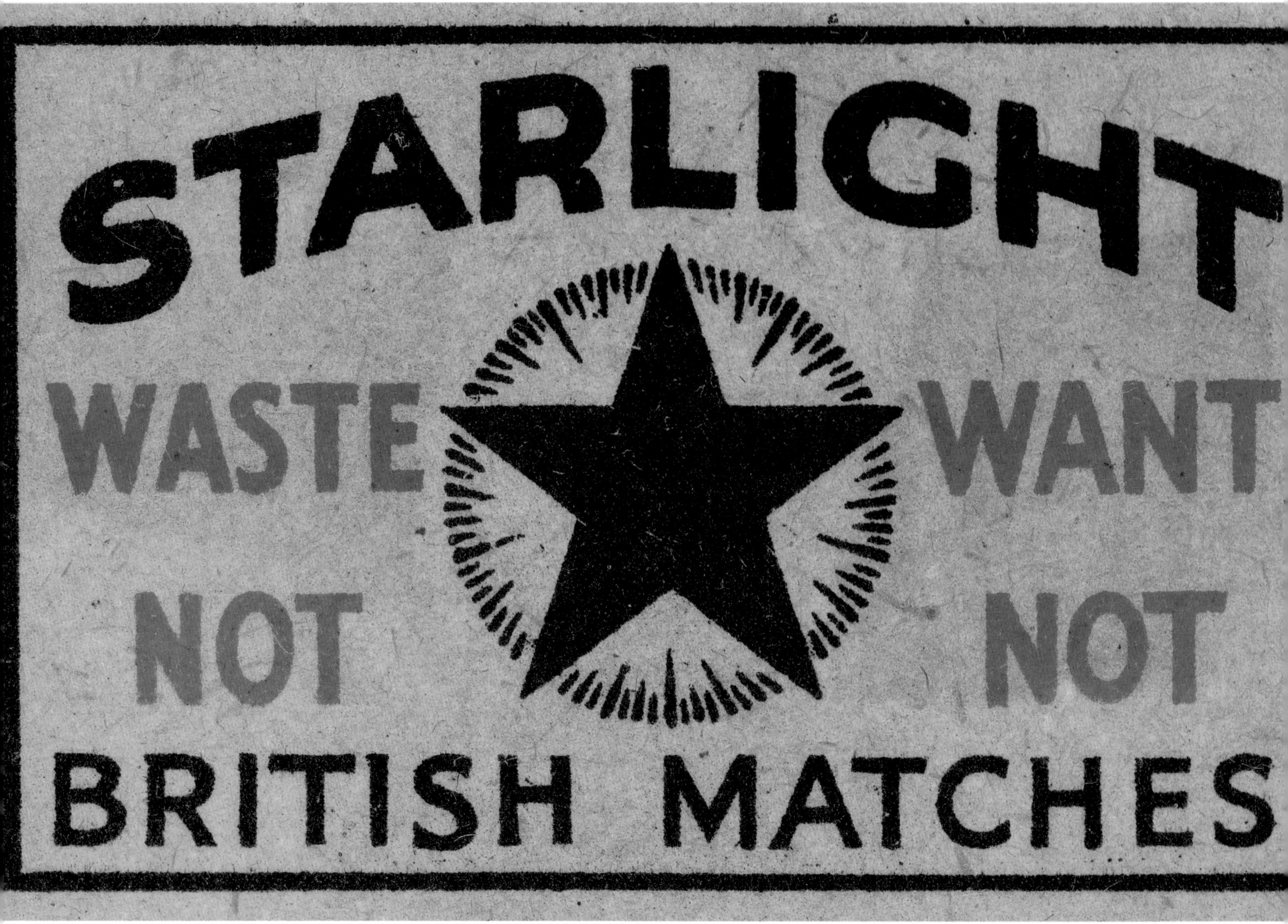
STARLIGHT
WASTE NOT
WANT NOT
BRITISH MATCHES

Chapter Ten

Mass Communication Matchboxes

These British labels from the second world war carry a strong message for fuel economy.

By the 1920s the safety match was well and truly established as a necessary part of daily life, even in the most remote parts of the globe. It would be fair to say that in some communities matches were vital, even precious, while in others they were just another convenience, an accepted part of household paraphernalia.

Yet already, in much of Europe for example, gas lighting was slowly but surely being replaced by electricity. Not so for vast populations in rural Asia and Africa where the open flame was still the primary source of light, heat and cooking.

The match industry was established. The major companies were investing, consolidating, expanding, refining. Global partnerships were being formed, rivalries intensified. These same companies, and the brands they represented, had quite literally become household names, their products handled by millions, many times a day.

What a great way to communicate!

Match makers had already learned by now that their customers took note of what was on the box label, and that potential was being recognised as a powerful means of message-carrying.

It was not just commercial enterprises that were to take advantage of this new medium. Governments were quick to recognise that this was a way to get into people's homes- and heads – with messages that could be both positive and political.

As a means of delivering propaganda, the matchbox had no equal at the time. Cheaper than a newspaper, sold in greater volume and with more repetitive use (a ratio of about fifty to one), the matchbox message would also reach illiterate audiences through simple imagery.

Both the first and second world wars saw the matchbox as a vehicle for messages, some positive, some patriotic. Most of the governments of countries involved in the conflict issued labels of this type, particularly during World War Two. Messages such as 'Dig for Victory', 'Don't Talk About Ships' or 'Careless Talk Costs Lives' could be found on matchboxes from Canada, USA, South Africa and India. Similar themes were current in France, Belgium and Holland, while

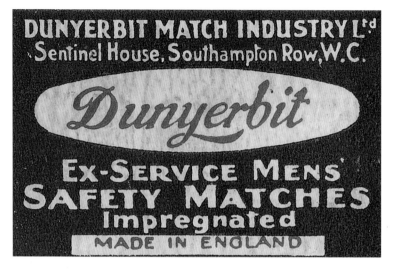

The matchbox as an effective propaganda source. The Czech label (above) urges people not to waste, while the post-war British label (above right) promotes fund-raising for ex-servicemen. During the second world war Austria's Solo Match Company was annexed by the German match monopoly and obliged to produce these boxes bearing Hitler's notorious slogan.

those from Japan tended to be more stirring and warlike. In Britain, Moreland's 'England's Glory' brand carried a variety of patriotic slogans which urged people not to waste, or promoting the need for fire safety awareness. Masters' 'Army and Navy' brand carried the message 'Matches are precious – make them last' during the war years, while Germany, having annexed the Austrian match industry just prior to World War Two, was able to produce and freely distribute Hitler's 'Ein Volk, Ein Reich, Ein Führer' slogan on its' matchboxes.

After both wars, various labels commemorated military heroes or acts of heroism, and sites of great battles. Some appealed to match buyers to remember the sacrifices made by the armed forces and to support disabled ex-servicemen, their organisations, the Red Cross or rebuilding programmes. Memorable among these are the Belgian 'Remember' brand – 'the disabled soldiers and sailors match' – and the British 'Dunyerbit' label.

'Don't waste food!' and 'Recycle!' were stern warnings on post-war Czech labels.

In the Soviet bloc countries of eastern Europe, and communist China, the number of post-war labels promoting Communist party ideals and celebrating glorious milestones of the revolution in industry, education or agriculture, must run into millions. The population was encouraged at all times to support the regime, while in the west various political parties gently encouraged the electorate to vote their way on polling day. 'Votez Libéral', a Belgian label bluntly states.

Not all governmental use of the matchbox as a means of communication was self-serving propaganda.

Information about health, or education, was and still is frequently dispensed via the matchbox to this day, particularly in rural areas in communities where literacy is low and the use of matches high. A study carried out by the Société Nationale des Allumettes in Madagascar, for example, where the open hearth is still the focus of daily life, revealed that one match was passed around up to five times before being extinguished and the matchbox put away.

In the mid 1970s the government of the Côte d'Ivoire (Ivory Coast), in a major effort to combat the country's

A label from the East African Match Co. of Kenya promoting Jomo Kenyatta's Kenya Education fund; forest fire awareness from Algeria; flood relief appeal from Holland. The Belgian electoral label canvassing liberal votes could not be clearer.

LE BOXEUR

Sven-Åke Lundbäck

SPOLA KRÖKEN =man dricker litet mindre och mår mycket bättre

KOOPT EEN GOED BOEK!

DRINKT GEEN ALCOHOL.

BE ON YOUR GUARD CARELESS TALK COSTS LIVES

Above: British wartime label. Top: the boxer from the Côte d'Ivoire fell victim to a government literacy campaign, while labels from Sweden (top left) and Holland (top right) carry anti-alcohol messages.

high level of illiteracy, introduced an imaginative scheme in cooperation with the local match manufacturer SOTROPAL (Société Tropicale des Allumettes). The University of Abidjan was called in to collaborate with graphics and phonetics, and a long series of matchbox labels was produced linking letters of the alphabet with familiar daily objects. The first labels, which replaced the popular 'Le Boxeur' brand of the time, showed a large letter of the alphabet in the centre, with a smaller picture and the word in full in top and bottom corners. The next version had all this mounted on a blackboard and easel, as if in a classroom. But this too was revised after the first issue to feature the picture and first letter of the subject described enlarged, centre label, and framed as if on a TV screen. This made the images appear more recognisable, for although literacy was low even the most remote communities had a TV set (see page 109). The impact of this campaign

was highly successful, and it remained in production for many years. So far the alphabet set is known to have appeared in over sixty varieties and is a good example of similar educational communications campaigns using the matchbox in a number of countries. Learning the alphabet via matchboxes was promoted in Venezuela and El Salvador, but it is probably the African continent that has seen the widest use of the matchbox as a means of communicating educational or public service information to the masses.

Just a few of the varied and vital topics covered included a leprosy awareness programme and a promotional campaign for decimal currency, both in Zambia; a child nutrition awareness programme in Ethiopia; a label from Kenya's East African Match Company featuring Jomo Kenyatta's appeal for support for the Kenya Education Fund; series of labels issued in Algeria promoting fire safety, health and hygiene, the national

census and road safety, with Libya also issuing road safety labels.

Indeed road safety and the highway code have been heavily promoted on matchboxes since the beginning of the great age of motoring, with increasingly long sets of labels being issued showing road signs and various ways of having accidents around the world as the number of vehicles on the roads, and the number of accidents, has increased. One of the earliest, from England, shows a motor car being preceded by a flag-waving policeman warning people to keep out of the way. Britain produced several road safety labels in later years, including those on the reverse of J.John Masters 'Army and Navy' boxes. France, Germany, Israel, China, Poland, Switzerland, Hungary, Australia and the Netherlands are just some of the countries whose governments have chosen the matchbox to promote this subject.

Labels promoting the national lotteries of Israel (top left) and Hungary (left). The heroic figure on the parlour-size box from the USA, dated February 1916 (above, centre), is King No-to-Bac, who, according to the legend on his shield, kills tobacco. One of the earliest examples of anti-smoking propaganda, it contrasts starkly with the Bulgarian anti-smoking label at top right.

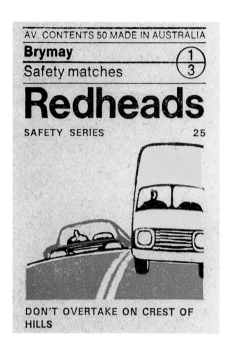

AV. CONTENTS 50 MADE IN AUSTRALIA
Brymay
Safety matches ①③
Redheads
SAFETY SERIES 25

DON'T OVERTAKE ON CREST OF HILLS

PRAWIDŁOWO UMOCOWANA LAMPA

61 Z PZ BYSTRZYCA PRZEC 64 ZAP 25 GR. PN SB10-94061

ZAPOBIEGA WYPADKOM

FIGYELJ

Road safety labels from (clockwise) Hungary, Australia, and Poland and (opposite) China, France and Algeria.

Encouraging people to take part in their country's national lottery was another popular government pastime. Belgium, France, Portugal, Bulgaria, Germany, Hungary, Israel and the former Yugoslavia have all issued lottery labels, while investment and money-saving schemes have featured in UK, Australia and former Czechoslovakia. Still on the theme of money, the introduction of decimal currency in Australia and UK (as well as Zambia) prompted public information labels. The protection of wildlife also featured prominently on labels from Czechoslovakia, as well as from Australia among several others.

All kinds of health and safety messages have been carried on matchboxes, often featuring, for example, infant vaccination programmes or messages about hygiene. Italian, South American, Australian and Swiss match companies have all issued this type of label, and government warnings against alcohol abuse have appeared in Sweden, Belgium, India and the Netherlands. The French government, on the other hand, via its state match monopoly, strongly encouraged wine consumption on its labels in the 1950s.

Of more relevance to match users were probably the many labels issued in various countries carrying fire safety warnings against the careless use of matches or cigarettes. Australia, Poland, USA, Lithuania and France figure among these. Anti-smoking messages, by way of a contrast, were comparatively rare, although a particularly graphic anti-smoking label was issued in Bulgaria.

Probably the oldest anti-smoking message on a matchbox is that on a rare old box issued in early 1916 in the USA. It shows the sword-wielding, gladiator-like character King No-to-bac. His shield carries the powerful warning 'No-to-bac Kills Tobacco'.

Many governments encouraged fundraising for charities through indirect contributions via state-owned match sales, while ongoing national schemes were sometimes stimulated by match manufacturers themselves – notably the Swedish Match Company's 'Sun Match Boy' programme described earlier. Disaster relief featured prominently on labels from the Netherlands and USA, particularly for flood victims.

With key brands established and mass production techniques becoming more and more refined, the art that was once inherent and intrinsic to matchbox label design of the early twentieth century was on the decline by World War Two, with a few enduring exceptions. Art was making way for design.

Wildlife conservation messages from Czechoslovakia.

Opposite page: decimal currency conversion message (Australia, 1966); post-war charity label, Belgium (top), and below, this German label warns train drivers against drinking on duty.

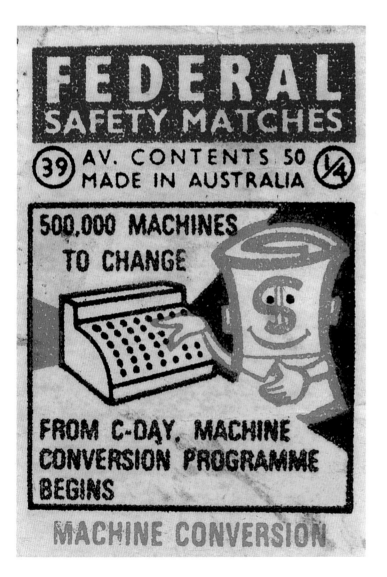

FEDERAL
SAFETY MATCHES
39 AV. CONTENTS 50 ¼
MADE IN AUSTRALIA

500,000 MACHINES
TO CHANGE

FROM C-DAY, MACHINE
CONVERSION PROGRAMME
BEGINS

MACHINE CONVERSION

IMPREGNATED
SAFETY MATCHES
REMEMBER
THE DISABLED
SOLDIERS' AND SAILORS' MATCH

AVERAGE 45 STICKS

MADE IN BELGIUM

Halt!
IM DIENST
KEINEN
ALKOHOL!

Labels from communist eastern Europe frequently evoked bold industrial and revolutionary images, like these examples from the Soviet Union of the 1950s and 1970s.

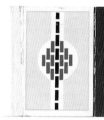

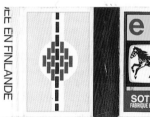

The evolution of a literacy campaign introduced by the government of the Côte d'Ivoire is shown here on these labels from SOTROPAL of Abidjan. The earliest examples (dark yellow) gave way to the paler ones, with the letters of the alphabet placed on a blackboard to represent learning. But putting the images on to a TV screen proved much more popular and effective. Note the printing along the edge of the modern cardboard boxes, showing that the card had to be imported from Finland.

TIGRA

TABALUX

Chapter Eleven

The Matchbox Goes Commercial

Left: A typical Belgian advertising label of the 1950s.
Above, a more recent Portuguese label combines an ad for soft drinks with a wildlife set for collectors.

Right from the beginning there had been an awareness of the advertising potential offered by the matchbox. Partly stimulated by novelty value and partly by a production process that permitted manufacturers to put their own name on one side of the box and sell the other panel to an advertiser, the early vesta boxes particularly were carrying a variety of advertising by the end of the nineteenth century.

To start with it was fairly localised, often publicising the importer of cigars, tobaccos and fancy goods who had sold the matches. Sometimes match boxes of this era carried advertising card inserts, but these quickly disappeared in favour of advertisers' 'own brand' boxes. Nevertheless it was still to be some time before advertising matches were to play a major role in manufacturers' output, and during the boom years of European match production in the first part of the twentieth century matchbox label content was dominated by attractive, colourful and artistic designs and motifs intended to attract highly diverse

audiences to buying matches. Establishing that habit was to take a few decades, but once it was the prospect of selling other products via the matchbox didn't seem so alien.

To advertisers the appeal of reaching domestic mass markets was as strong as it was for governments in education or in spreading propaganda. In countries where match manufacture was state controlled some national products and industries enjoyed a free ride, but globally advertisers recognised the value in the volume of production and frequency of use of the matchbox as an outlet – and manufacturers saw an additional source of revenue.

By the turn of the century matchboxes were already carrying advertising for soap, custard, hats, whisky and assorted miracle pills. Eventually there was to be no limit to the variety of products and services advertised on matchboxes. With matchbox labels now being predominantly single panel size, the evocative and colourful artworks that brought so much diversity to such a mundane object as the matchbox began quite

Early advertising labels featured the necessities of life: whisky, metal polish, pickles and tea.

rapidly to be displaced by the sales slogans and logos of a multitude of marketeers. True, a number of key brands survived the centuries, being modernised and modified en route. A few classic examples are Ship, Three Stars, Swallow and Flower Basket from Sweden; Three Torches from Belgium; Swan, England's Glory and Bryant & May's Ark from Britain; Welt-Hölzer from Germany; Key and Scissors from Czechoslovakia; Independence and Diamond from USA; Redheads from Australia and Lion from South Africa. So as match makers and distributors realised the value to them of own-brand advertising matches for customers, new areas of sales were opened up.

It was to be a development which both boosted existing manufacturers' sales and threatened them with the creation of intense competition from newly-formed match companies created solely for advertising sales purposes, and from the book match.

To advertise on matchboxes customers could either go to local manufacturers, who were increasingly willing to sell space on their boxes for advertisers' labels, or to match importers and distributors who would be bringing matches in bulk from overseas markets for local labelling. This is how some popular brands came to be made in a number

of different countries over the years as importers and distributors switched their sources of supply.

Another trend to develop, which remains popular to this day on the modern, label-less all-printed cardboard boxes known as 'skillets' is the on-box prize promotion or competition, designed to boost sales either of the matches – or the product advertised on the box. The first promotion of this kind can be traced back to the early 1900s, and offered in its range of prizes everything from a jam spoon to a motor car as incentives.

Labels like these were common in Britain in the 1950s and 60s.

Much of the earliest matchbox advertising reflected similar trends around the world, with the same kinds of products being predominant: tea and coffee, beer and whisky, soaps, washing powders and disinfectants, pipes, cigarettes, cigars and tobacco. Soon, almost every pub, hotel and restaurant was to have its own label, along with motor car and bicycle makers and airlines. Once stability had returned after the second world war and economies were regenerating, every conceivable product or service was being advertised on matchboxes, and by now advertisers and distributors' labels almost outnumbered those of manufacturers' own brands.

As far as label design goes this was generally bad news, as advertising labels would often be wordy and drab. A label from Hong Kong of the time just said 'Please Try On Lok Yuen's Ice Cream'. An equally terse Indian label implored movie goers to 'See Jawab at Imperial'.

Typical of advertising labels seen in Britain in the 1950s were Czech imports for Skol and Double Diamond beers which just showed the respective company logos. Maid Marian Foods, 3 Hands Disinfectant, Martin (newsagents), and Lewis of Westminster (tobacconists) were all common own brand advertising labels, but not all lacked creativity. The now-defunct *Evening News* newspaper promoted itself on matchboxes with an amusing set of cartoons, as did National petrol.

Indeed cartoons were – and still are – a popular way of attracting attention to matchbox ads. In Germany the Allianz insurance company's matchbox label cartoons have been a way of life for years as have those of the Rewe supermarket chain. Holland's advertisers also had a sense of humour, with Spar supermarkets and Mascotte cigarette papers issuing sets of cartoons while Vivo supermarkets offered a set of circus scenes. Rizla, cigarette paper makers, issued a number of sets advertising their products, with themes which included cars, birds and national flags.

Advertising in eastern Europe pre-Glasnost was a less colourful and varied business, being restricted to nationalised or government enterprises such as truck, tractor or car factories, heavy industry or the national airline. Not so in Belgium, where own brand advertising labels had been proliferating since the 1930s.

The number of labels coming out of Belgium in the years immediately before and after world war two was quite high for a small country, with companies such as Union Match and La Nationale Independante turning out an astonishing variety for both local and export markets.

While many were of uninspiring content, they were at least part of the way of life. They related to everyday items and activities, and were themselves part of the domestic consumer process. Not all were unattractive. A

series for Waeslandia groceries, while old-fashioned in style, was a colourful, albeit rather formal, display on paper of the company's goods. More varied and colourful were the many labels and sets of labels printed for various cigarette companies. Belga offered a nice set of glamour girls, and rivals Sprint showed racing cyclists (a very popular subject in Belgium), racing cars and motor bikes. Armada cigarettes later sponsored a colourful set of labels for the 1958 Brussels World Fair showing national costumes from around the

Cartoons were popular in matchbox label advertising, like these from Germany's Allianz Insurance, and the London Evening News (opposite) and National petrol (above).

REWE Schmunzelwitz No. 0052

Cartoon labels for Holland's Mascotte cigarette papers, Rewe supermarkets (Germany) and Spar supermarkets (Holland).

Rewe Schmunzelwitz No. 0036

world. VéGé supermarkets meanwhile went for lengthy sets of national flags and cars , while the Belgian division of the Ford Motor Company promoted its 1957 model range on matchboxes.

Next-door neighbours France, while having a far greater population, was less prolific, probably because the match industry was a state monopoly. Nevertheless, a few French labels of the time stand out, notably the Gitanes cigarettes gypsy girls, and some attractive early labels promoting Algerian dates, Ford cars and Automoto bicycles.

French labels often carry a capital letter in one corner. This identifies the particular factory that made the matches and there are about twenty possible varieties. Similarly, in Germany, the factory of origin is identified by a number and there are over forty known varieties.

Finnish domestic advertising labels very much reflected the trends of the time throughout western Europe, with supermarkets, garages, hotels and restaurants featuring strongly. In common with India, however, Finland was to produce a quantity of promotional labels for films.

During its relatively short life in the early 1950s the South African Match Company produced vast numbers of customer labels under its Phoenix brand , but even this was not enough to sustain sales and it closed in 1955. No such misfortune for Portugal's Sociedade Nacional de Fósforos, which offered a wide range of labels for advertisers to sponsor. Companies like Valentine (paints) or Superfresco soft drinks added their names to long lines of labels featuring, for example, animals or birds.

Brazil's booming match industry also saw a wide range of advertising labels appear, while manufacturers' own brands stayed strong. In the USA some of the best-known advertising labels included Tampa Nugget and Hav-a-Tampa for that brand of cigar.

Belgian advertising labels for coffee (top), and beer.

SAFETY MATCHES
TAUNUS 15 M 1957

Ford Motor Company
(BELGIUM)

SAFETY MATCHES
LINCOLN
PREMIÈRE LANDAU 1957

Ford Motor Company
(BELGIUM)

MERCKX MATCH
MADE IN BELGIUM
Ph. Merckx
VOEDINGSWAREN
VOEDINGSWAREN
ST. JAN BERCHMANSSTRAAT 108-110
MECHELEN · TEL : 136.02.

Belgium produced an astonishing variety of advertising labels in the 1950s and 60s, like these for 1957 Ford cars (top and centre, above), Merckx groceries, (above), and countless brands of cigarettes, tobacco, cigars, beer and coffee.

tabac
WELTA
tabak

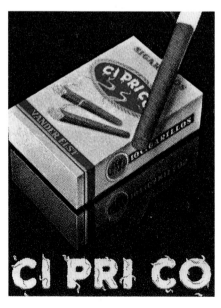

CI PRI CO

BELGA
VANDER ELST

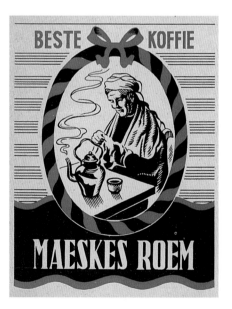

BESTE KOFFIE

MAESKES ROEM

An attractive series of labels showing the Waeslandia grocery chain's products, and two labels from a colourful Armada cigarettes set promoting Belgium's 1958 World Fair.

Belgian advertising labels are varied and colourful.

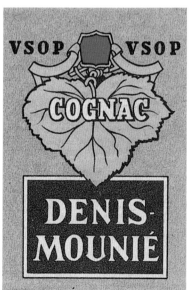

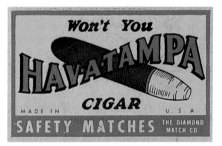

Clockwise: Belgian advertisement for cognac; 1958 Brussels World Fair label; American cigar advertising from Diamond Match; Portuguese paint; South African fish & chips.

French labels frequently have a capital letter in one corner denoting factory of origin, while German labels have a factory number. The number 30 on the Familien-Feuerzeug box from about 1910 denotes the excise number, while number 23 on the Konsumhölzer is the manufacturing company's membership number of the German Safety Match Convention (1905-1909).

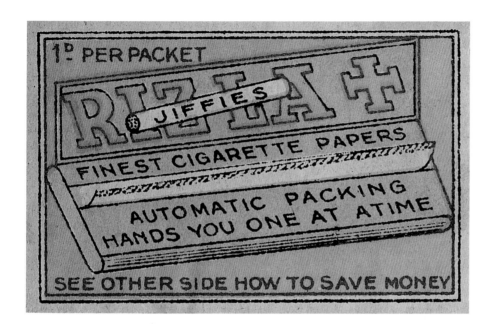

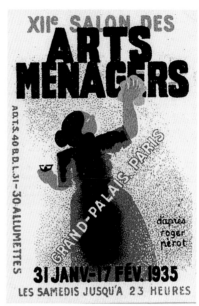

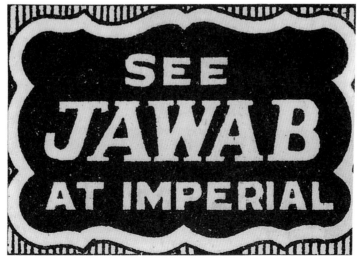

Clockwise, from top left: British cigarette paper advertising; French label for a 1935 Paris exhibition; Indian cinema label; circus set for a Dutch supermarket.

Chapter Twelve

Boom or Burnout?

*An exrplosive theme from
South Africa's Capital
Match Korp., 1998*

The years between the wars were boom years for match makers. The huge demand for matches stimulated global expansion of the match industry, which spread rapidly through the combination of agent and distributor networks, investment in local plant and acquisition of or partnership with local manufacturers. Add to this a new accessibility to vast and hitherto remote populations and an enormous increase in smoking and we're talking about a hot property.

Competition and rivalry between manufacturers was intense, yet was to lead to collaboration in the need to combat dumping of cheaper, inferior products that were threatening to undermine the market which had to unify and strengthen to survive.

The machinery of the match industry was also evolving, making way for safer and more efficient production, and the technology has changed little since the introduction of the now-standard continuous process, originally introduced in Sweden in 1864.

Whether the second world war was a contributory factor in the dramatic downturn of fortune that was to affect the match business of the 1950s is questionable, but there is no doubt that by the middle of the twentieth century match sales were to see first a substantial decline, then a virtual standstill. The war was certainly responsible for serious shortages of raw materials worldwide. Every country had prior demands for timber, chemicals and the other essential elements for match manufacture. Rationing hit other materials, notably fuel, which in turn affected transport and delivery of matches, shipping having suffered heavily as a result of war activity anyway. While there existed an apparently huge demand for matches during the war years it was in fact one caused by shortages that could not be met rather than growing consumption. The Korean war was to compound the situation, particularly in Asia.

There were other contributing factors to the sales slump, leading in turn to the changes in the match industry which have made the once-common colourful matchbox label a relative scarcity today. The downward trend in volume sales continued, as daily life itself changed and evolved globally.

Modern, label-less matchboxes.

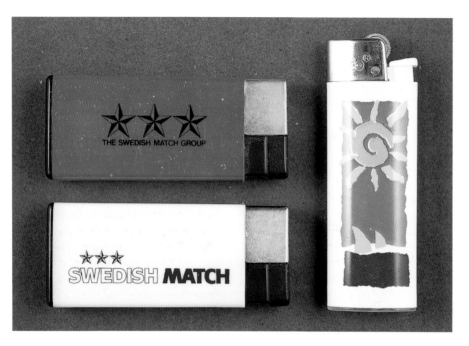

The growth and popularity of cheap, disposable lighters often given away free as promotional items had a major impact on match sales, forcing some manufacturers of traditional matches to diversify into lighter production.

The technology of the naked flame is being superseded, and with it the match too.

Of course this does not apply to less developed regions and remote parts of Africa, Asia, South America – even Europe – yet. An enormous decline in smoking in the so-called developed world has also been a significant contributor to declining match sales. Dedicated smokers tend to use lighters anyway.

In an effort to combat their own declining sales, cigarette manufacturers targeted highly-populous third-world countries with high volume sales potential and less stringent anti-smoking policies. Yet in countries where the use of matches was generally high, lighters were perceived as a fashionable luxury accessory – so cigarette manufacturers, and often other makers of consumer goods, distributed free, disposable lighters.

Regardless of this, the disposable lighter was a hugely popular item around the world anyway, and mirrored the match in being a cheap and efficient source of fire. They soon became equally colourful and equally effective as a marketing medium.

Seeing sales of matches stagnate, major manufacturers were forced to diversify. The disposable lighter business was to be a logical part of this diversification, and ultimately

Some of the changes were part of that same industrial evolution to which the match itself belonged, but to which it would fall victim.

In most of the world, electric lighting has completely replaced candle or gas light in homes, workplaces and street lighting. Where it hasn't yet, it soon will. Increasingly, microwave ovens and electric cookers are replacing open fires and gas-powered stoves, and where gas remains in use it often comes with electronic ignition. Central heating is now the norm rather than the coal fire, and also provides the hot water.

Swedish Match was to become a major producer, while Bryant & May a key global distributor

While this diversification may have provided an extra boost to business, it did nothing for match sales, and in fact contributed to their continuing decline.

It was not the only thing. Even before the development of the giveaway, throwaway promotional lighter, post war consumerism and the consequent advertising boom that accompanied it had spawned another rival to the traditional box of matches and its label – the giveaway advertising match.

While the match industry initially enjoyed the rewards of the high demand for advertising labels, the combination of new marketing methods and new technology was to work against it and accelerate the decline of the manufacturer's own matchbox label.

The ongoing refinement of the continuous manufacturing process meant that the making of matchboxes was quicker, cleaner and simpler. Disappearing fast were the days of matchbox sleeve held in shape and glued together with blue paper wrapper, tray similarly assembled, and a separately-printed label pasted on top.

Now tray and sleeve were made of card, folded and brought together by machines which also painted on the striking strip and applied glue at the join. The manufacturer's brand, trade mark or image was printed straight on to the card. No more need for a label.

For most producers who could afford to upgrade their machinery the new process made life much easier by eliminating elements such as wood and paper, replacing them with sheets of card. As long as supplies were available, that is. Uniquely, Sudan's Modern Match Producing and Distributing Company switched to this method of production relatively late, in 1972, but due to demand and shortages of ink were unable to cope with the printing of the card. So locally-produced Sudanese matchboxes were completely plain for some time.

Another type of match industry was now developing. Using the improved production methods, new specialist advertising match companies were being set up to provide customers with quick delivery, own-design boxes, mostly as free giveaway promotional items. These mini boxes, as they came to be called, containing only a dozen or twenty matches, could come in any variety of design, and with a laminated finish. In reality the companies supplying these advertising boxes were acting as agents for match manufacturers, the matches themselves being imported from various sources. The difference now is that instead of bearing labels the boxes are custom-printed, with invariably less imaginative artwork or design than their paper labelled predecessors, and the matches come mainly from Japan.

For almost half a century the free advertising mini box has grown in global popularity, to the benefit of the new breed of ad match distributors and at the expense of the traditional manufacturers and their labels.

Yet the biggest impact of all over the past century, despite a slow start, is probably that made by the match book – although book matches today must also compete with the disposable lighter and free advertising match, as well as with their long-time rival, the traditional box of wooden safety matches.

The match book was first patented in the United States in 1892 by one Joshua Pusey. Quite rightly, he reckoned that smokers would prefer the slimmer, lighter, easier-to-carry packaging of the match book to the traditional box of matches, which in those days was generally larger than today's modern box.

Initial interest was high, but rapidly dwindled because, like those early wooden matches, the first generation of book matches simply wasn't safe. Book match production started

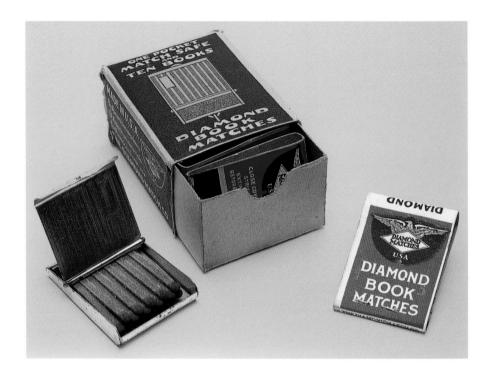

in Britain in about 1899 because of Bryant & May's association with the Diamond Match Company of America, who had acquired Pusey's patent. It was a slow start, but by the 1920s, once the quality issue was sorted out, match books were being produced – and given away – by the billion.

Match book production started out – and remains – a US-dominated industry, and while it too has seen a dramatic downturn for reasons that mirror those suffered by the safety match industry, it today represents the free distribution of literally billions of giveaway advertising booklets promoting every conceivable type of product or service. The advertising match cover comes in countless sizes and imaginative shapes, sometimes with the advertisers' message printed on the matches themselves, and the use of book matches vastly exceeds that of wooden safety matches.

ДЕРЕВЯННОЕ ЗОДЧЕСТВО

КОГДА–ТО ВСЯ РУСЬ БЫЛА ДЕРЕВЯННОЙ. ОТ БЕЛОГО МОРЯ И ДО ЧЕРНОГО НА РУСИ ВОЗВОДИЛИ КРЕПОСТИ
И ОСТРОГИ, ДВОРЦЫ И ИЗБЫ, ЧАСОВНИ И МОНАСТЫРИ, МЕЛЬНИЦЫ И АМБАРЫ, МОСТЫ И КОЛОДЦЫ, РУССКАЯ
ДЕРЕВЯННАЯ АРХИТЕКТУРА – ЭТО НЕОТЪЕМЛЕМАЯ СОСТАВНАЯ ЧАСТЬ ВСЕЙ ОТЕЧЕСТВЕННОЙ ХУДОЖЕСТВЕННОЙ
КУЛЬТУРЫ. ВОТ ПОЧЕМУ ДРАГОЦЕННО ДЛЯ НАС ЗАМЕЧАТЕЛЬНОЕ НАСЛЕДИЕ НАРОДНОЙ АРХИТЕКТУРЫ,
СОХРАНИВШЕЙСЯ В КАРЕЛИИ, АРХАНГЕЛЬСКОЙ, МУРМАНСКОЙ, ВОЛОГОДСКОЙ, КОСТРОМСКОЙ ОБЛАСТЯХ
И ПОДМОСКОВЬЕ.

1. Новгородский музей народного зодчества. 2. Кижи. Часовня из деревни Лёликозеро. Памятник архитектуры XVII–XVIII в.в. 3. Кижи. Часовня из деревни Выгово. Памятник архитектуры XVII–XVIII в.в.
4. Кижи. Волкостровская часовня. 5. Кижи. Часовня. Памятник архитектуры XIV в. 6. Памятник архитектуры XVII в. из
села Микишево. Новгородский музей народного зодчества 7. Памятник архитектуры XVII в. на реке Ишне Ярославской обл. 8. Памятник архитектуры XVII в. из села
Варзуга Мурманской обл. 9. Дом А. М. Бусырева из деревни Конюшенская Вологодской обл. 10. Мель-
ница-шатровка из деревни Кожпоселок Архангельской обл. 11. Шатровая мельница из села Кочемлева.
Музей деревянного зодчества в Истре. Подмосковье 12. Мельница – "столбовка" 13. Изба начала XIX в.
Новгородский музей народного зодчества 14. Памятник архитектуры XVII в. из села Кушерека Архангельской обл. 15. Колокольня из деревни Кулига. Начало XVII в. Архангельская обл. 16. Дом в Теру-
сельге, Вологодская обл. 17. Ветряная мельница в деревне Мстонь Новгородской обл. 18. Кижи. Ветряная мельница из деревни Волкостров 19. Мельница. XVII в. Новгородский музей народного зодчества
20. Усадьба Кокориных из бывшей деревни Выхино. Музей деревянного зодчества в Истре. Подмосковье
21. Кижи. Памятник архитектуры XVII–XIX в.в. из деревни Кивгора 22. Кижи. Памятник архитектуры
XVIII–XIX в.в. из деревни Воробьи 23. Дом середины XIX в. из села Юксовичи Новгородской обл.
24. Памятник архитектуры XVII в. из деревни Вершины Архангельской обл. 26. Памятник архитектуры
25. Памятник архитектуры XVII в. из села Семёновское. Музей деревянного зодчества в Истре.
XVIII в. из села Сокольники. Музей деревянного зодчества г. Иркутск 27. Памятник
деревянного зодчества г. Иркутск 28. Надвратная башня ограды Николо-Карельского монастыря XVII в.
Коломенское. Москва

Chapter Thirteen

Sets Appeal

Sets for collectors were introduced to boost stagnating match sales. An attractive and popular example is 'Folklore Scenes' (above). Boxed sets for tourists were popular in the USSR. Pictured left is one from 1980 featuring traditional wooden buildings.

After surviving the war years the match industry enjoyed a brief resurgence, but since the early 1950s has seen traditional wooden match sales steadily decline. The combination of diminished sales volume and modern box production means that the rich variety of matchbox labels that was once so common is also fast declining, and although some advertising match companies still offer customers own-label boxes they generally lack the creativity and imagination of their predecessors. There are, of course, exceptions, notably among the cottage industries of Asia and smaller factories in the sub-continent, Africa and South America where the new production techniques have yet to be employed and which are still a rich source of labels – in quantity, if not in quality.

Another inevitable move that match makers made to protect profits was to slowly but surely reduce the number of matches in a box. Prewar boxes of sixty matches might have cost a penny (about ¹/₂ a new penny). By the 1960s the content was down to thirty and the price was up to 2d. (about 1p). After decimalisation in 1971 it remained at 1p for thirty matches, but by 1980 the price of 38 Bryant & May matches was 3p. Today a box of forty matches can cost 15p.

With importers sourcing their matches from various countries, and boxes carrying information such as country of origin, number of contents and price on their labels, collectors could find considerable numbers of varieties of the same label or brand over the years, particularly between the 1950s and the 1980s.

In an effort to boost stagnant sales, match makers – and particularly distributors – turned. To a new tactic to try and keep the public buying their matches: long and colourful sets of labels meant to attract both consumers and collectors.

The big names in the match industry tended to keep out of this practice. Although they had initiated the first sets and series of multi-coloured and glazed labels at the beginning of the twentieth century, the major Swedish, Austrian and British companies preferred to support and sustain sales of their well-known and well-established key brands.

Today it seems a pity that those high quality miniatures, with their images of fashion, folklore and circus, or Indian maharajahs and military gentlemen, are no longer produced.

The well-known Camp flags set from Belgium came in many varieties during the 1960s and 70s.

The products of the great sales drive of the mid-twentieth century were rather more mundane compared to the glorious images of earlier times, although far from lacking in variety.

True, some sets had appeared in Britain ahead of the wave to come. J.John Masters had produced a series of military badges during the second world war, followed by a road safety series and a set of commonwealth emblems, among others. Bryant & May produced a lengthy series of shipping company insignia, which also served as advertising labels.

The craze for sets began to take hold in the 1960s and then exploded in the '70s and '80s.

Bearing in mind the difficulties of the match industry at the time, the production of long sets of labels seems to be a rather illogical marketing move given the cost of originating and printing so many different images and so many varieties of labels. Nevertheless, it happened, much to the joy of collectors. But in the long run they were to be the only beneficiaries. The gains made by importers and distributors and various manufacturers, mostly European, represented only a temporary upswing in match sales.

In Eastern Europe, particularly since the establishment of the Soviet Union, enormous numbers of lengthy sets of matchbox labels have always been in evidence. Generally produced by state match monopolies their purpose was to promote and glorify government achievements, or cultural and sporting prowess.

Aimed at promoting awareness and morale in domestic markets rather than simply to boost sales, the variety is endless and ranges from rich and colourful scenes from the circus or ballet to images of dreary factories, collective farms or dams. Boxed sets for tourists were, and still are, always available at state gift shops and airports and depict everything from subway stations to national monuments (one and the same thing in Moscow), as well as theatres, museums and art treasures.

One of the most elaborate Russian sets was produced for the 1957 Moscow Youth Festival and comprised some four thousand labels in many different colours and designs. Another set, issued in 1966, commemorates the battles of 1941-45 in Leningrad, Volgograd, Sebastopol, Kiev, Moscow and Odessa among others, and in the same year a long sport set was produced.

These are but a few examples out of thousand produced in the former Soviet Union and, to a lesser extent, other Eastern bloc countries. The

Ne vendez jamais la peau de l'ours

avant de l'avoir tué

A père avare, fils prodigue

French labels of the 1960s were much enlivened by the issue of these sets of proverbs and fables. Also pictured (top right) is another variation on the popular Folklore Scenes theme.

L'ANE VETU DE LA PEAU DE LION

SEITA

SEITA

LE LION ET LE MOUCHERON

AVERAGE 33 FOREIGN MATCHES

BENZ 1895

The Belgian VéGé super-market chain issued a number of lengthy sets in different varieties which included flags, coats-of-arms, and locomotives. Most successful was the set of 60 vintage cars (above and opposite).

region remains a good source of labels despite the fragmentation of the USSR.

Sport and sporting occasions have always been matchbox label themes, particularly during Olympic Games or football World Cup years, and on these occasions their production was by no means limited to Eastern Europe.

In common with its communist neighbours, China became another vast source of sets of labels of all kinds, and with an enormous domestic market to satisfy. The charming, high-quality traditional art of early Chinese labels has long given way to simple labels of unbelievably dreary quality or garish sets of monuments, bridges, factories and dams. To be fair, however, there have also been numerous sets of attractive and colourful labels, but being mass produced, probably in millions, they are not highly rated by collectors.

At least one pretty set of butterfly labels was produced in 1979, and another, one hundred varieties long, featured wild flowers. Regularly reissued themes also include birds, wild animals and fish, and naturally enough the panda features frequently on Chinese labels, either solo or in sets.

Touristic highlights and natural wonders of Chinese provinces and cities are heavily promoted throughout the country, and have featured beauty spots in Fuzhou, Shanghai, Soochow, Jingchong, Tengchang, Nantong, Qindao, Suzhou and Kwongchow to name a few.

In stark contrast are more mundane sets featuring, of all things, drill bits, micrometers and torches, almost equalled for their bizarre contents by a set issued by the Czech Solo factory featuring different kinds of sausage meat.

At the other end of the spectrum are the colourful and interesting sets issued in Australia. Australia is one country whose match makers are well known for producing long sets of labels over the years. Usually numbering 40 or 64 labels in length, Australian match factories have applied 'sets appeal' to its maximum impact for both consumers and collectors.

The variety of subjects is broad, the quality of the artwork detailed. The Federal Match Co. (later to be acquired by Bryant & May) included in their output, among many others, a set of great explorers and their achievements, and a series of Australian regional emblems and coats-of-arms, reissued from time to time.

But it is certainly the countless number of labels to be produced

CROIX ROUGE INTERNATIONAL

INTERNATIONALE RODE KRUIS

VéGé

84

DUER 1907

SUNBEAM 1899

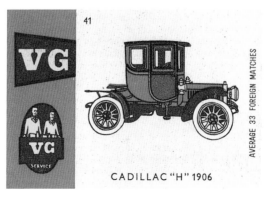

CADILLAC "H" 1906

AVERAGE 33 FOREIGN MATCHES

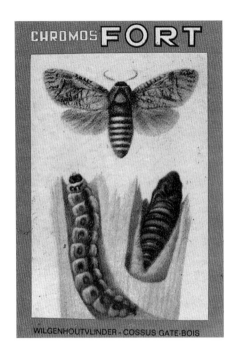

WILGENHOUTVLINDER - COSSUS GATE-BOIS

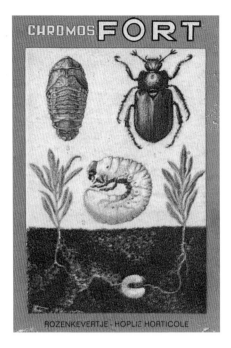

ROZENKEVERTJE - HOPLIE HORTICOLE

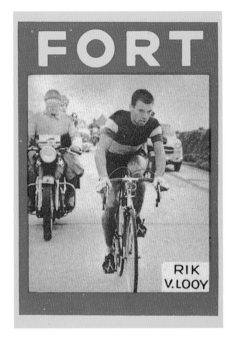

RIK V. LOOY

The Belgian Fort chain also issued numerous sets featuring all kinds of wildlife, as well as popular cycling heroes of the day.

93. — Kraagbeer - Ours à collier

British supermarket chains also discovered sets appeal. Pictured here are examples from ASDA's transport set, Safeways' birds and Sainsburys' vintage vehicles, all from 1987.

BRYMAY
Redheads ⅓
SAFETY MATCHES
AVERAGE CONTENTS 50 • MADE IN AUSTRALIA

No. 47

SCOTT REACHES
SOUTH POLE 1912

BRYMAY
Redheads ⅓
SAFETY MATCHES

STEPHENSON'S
"ROCKET",
1829

No. 30

AVERAGE CONTENTS 50
MADE IN AUSTRALIA

BRYMAY
Redheads ⅓
SAFETY MATCHES

FIRST BRYANT & MAY
SAFETY MATCH,
EARLY 19th CENTURY

No. 35

AVERAGE CONTENTS 50
MADE IN AUSTRALIA

H263

Redheads
CONTENTS 47 MATCHES
MADE IN AUSTRALIA. W.A. MATCH

AV. CONTENTS 50 MADE IN AUSTRALIA
W. A. Match Co.   15
Safety matches   1
Redheads

DINGO   19

H263

Redheads
CONTENTS 47 MATCHES
MADE IN AUSTRALIA. W.A. MATCH

Australia's 'Redheads' brand produced countless varieties of labels in sets covering a wide range of subjects.

*French labels of the
1960s featuring regional
costumes and space explo-
ration.*

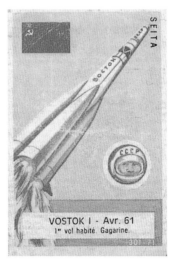

*Opposite page: cars pro-
vided an irresistible theme
for collectors' sets. The
Britannia Match series of
British Cars first
appeared in 1976 and
several other companies
issued sets on similar
themes.*

ARTHUR COOPER
(Wine Merchant) Ltd

AV. 50 FINNISH STICKS

SERIES OF 18 No. 7

14 H.P. ADAMS LANDAULETTE

CMC

under the famous 'Redheads' brand that are best known in Australia. Produced by Brymay (Bryant & May) and Western Australia Match Co., themes of some of the sets produced include Wonders of the World, inventors and their inventions, architecture, Greek mythology, fish, birds, flowers, fruit, marine life, transport, vintage cars, space, agriculture, safety, uniforms, costumes and many more.

Yet despite the ingenuity and creativity of its match companies, producing among the highest volume and variety of labels anywhere outside Eastern Europe, match sales continued to decline and Australians were to become among the most eager con-

verts to disposable lighters. Ironically this need was to be met by Bryant & May, who were to become one of the country's major suppliers.

In Europe, Austria's Solo Match Works was to be a major source of both direct exports and matches for distributors. One of Solo's early sets first appeared in Britain in 1959 and comprised a colourful set of ten flowers, ultimately available in at least half-a-dozen varieties. Many of the company's later sets were to be much longer.

One of these was the lengthy Cornish Wrecks series. Matches from Solo of Austria and later Finn-Match OY of Finland, were imported and

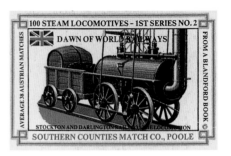

Southern Counties Match Co. issued their '100 Steam Locomotives' between 1976-1978.

distributed by Britain's Cornish Match Co. in their attractively-labelled boxes depicting famous ship-wrecks around the Cornish coastline. At least twelve sets were produced from Austria, and nine more from Finland, comprising three series of 69 different illustrations. Issued between 1967 and 1974 they provided quite a challenge to label collectors. The Cornish Match Co. produced a

number of other sets, including, in 1970, the 60-long Nursery Rhymes series, and the shorter Cornish Countryside set.

The Britannia Match Co. was another importer of Austrian matches to create several long sets, each of 100 different images. They were usually released in batches of 25. The first of these, issued in 1976, was a set of 100 British cars which eventually appeared in three varieties. In 1980 the company issued another attractive set of 100 British ships, followed in 1981 by a 100-long set entitled British Naval Ships. Britannia Match also issued a further set of 14 London Scenes which was to appear in two or three varieties.

Two other notable sets of labels were issued at about the same time by another importer of Austrian matches, the Southern Counties Match Co. Their '100 Steam Locomotives', issued between 1976-1978, is a colour-ful collectable in at least two varieties, as is their set of 60 British military uniforms.

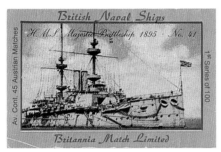

Examples from the long and varied 'Cornish Wrecks' series from Cornish Match, issued between 1967 and 1974. Britannia Match issued 'British Ships' (1980) and 'British Naval Ships' (1981).

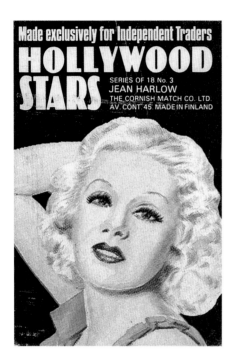
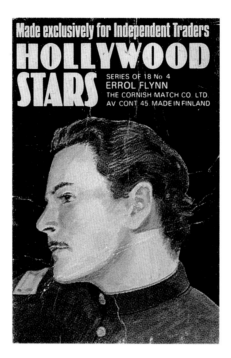
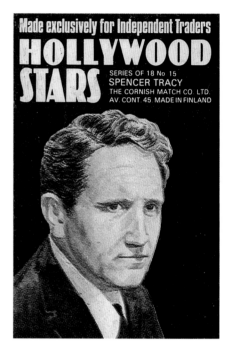

'Hollywood Stars' from the Cornish Match Co. (1982).

Belgium, with a competitive and diminishing match industry, was another source of sets for both the domestic and export markets, and produced some of the best-known. Among them was an extension of the popular 'Camp' brand, the Camp Flags of Nations sets. Issued in the 1960s and 1970s, there were three different sets of 20 national flags in a total of eleven varieties, some of which were also imported using Finnish matches.

Another popular Belgian issue was the set of 60 veteran cars pro-duced domestically for VéGé super-markets and exported under the VG brand. They exist in at least six known varieties. The domestic VéGé arm also issued a set of 100 national coats-of-arms for local consumption, as well as sets of flags and locomo-tives. Between the mid 1950s and the mid-1970s the Fort wholesale grocery chain issued about twenty-two known sets of over 250 labels of birds, poultry, ducks, insects, butterflies, fish, reptiles, animals and bats for the local market.

With its abundant supplies of

good quality timber Finland, like Sweden, was another major source of matches. Many were exported to distributors throughout Europe and provided another outlet for large sets of labels designed to boost sales. As in Belgium, Finland's match industry generated long sets of labels for both domestic and overseas sales.

The late 1970s and early 1980s saw considerable quantities of Finnish-sourced label sets appearing in export markets, particularly in Britain, although a number were also issued for domestic and regional distribution. These included sets of fish, butterflies and moths for sale in Finland, Denmark and Sweden, and a very long set of military uniforms for the local market. Several long sets of labels showing famous buildings around the world were issued between 1964-1974 for the Finnish and Danish markets.

In Britain, however, the number of distributors that sprang up and the number and variety of labels that appeared as a consequence was considerable, but while some of them flourished it was to be only a few years before another decline and the virtual disappearance of the matchbox with its label in favour of the printed cardboard box.

Companies including the Harrow Match Agency, Sussex Match Co., Southern Counties Match Co. and

Kentish Match Co. all distributed sets of matchboxes featuring assorted subjects on their labels such as castles, aircraft, windmills and wildlife, while the Britannia Match Co. distributed a number of sets entitles 'London Scenes', sourcing matches from Austria, USSR, Turkey and Yugoslavia. At least 14 varieties of this set are thought to have been produced, the various sets ranging in length from eight to 20 different images.

Of all the independent distributors, none was more prolific or creative than the Cornish Match Co., issuing colourful and collectable labels under their own name and for clients such as Finlays Newsagents, Lavells, Maynards and wine merchants Arthur Cooper.

In 1978 the company issued a set of eighteen Vintage Railway Engines. In 1980 there followed a set of 18 different dog breeds, which appeared eventually in three varieties, and in 1981 a set of tropical fish in two varieties. In the same year Cornish Match issued two more varied sets, one called Great British Castles the second Great British Cars. Almost invariably each set comprised 18 different images. 1982 saw the release of 'Cats' (three varieties), and 'Hollywood Stars'. Other notable issues from Cornish Match were to be Endangered Animals of the World

Austria's Solo Match Works first produced its flowers set in 1959.

紫花地丁
药用全草

77 20-7　南京火柴厂

南京长江大桥　上海火柴厂

上海火柴

Modern Chinese labels from long sets of butterflies, buildings and pandas. Below, one of a set of butterflies from Finland.

AVERAGE 50 CONTENT

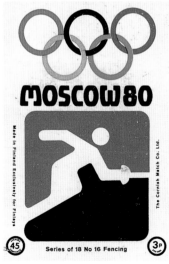

Major sporting events were always popular label themes like these from Germany for the 1956 Leipzig Sports Festival; 1984 Los Angeles Olympics (Cornish Match); 1982 World Cup (Cornish Match); 1968 Olympics (France); 1980 Olympics (Cornish Match); and 1972 Olympics (Germany).

Themes for sets were sometimes surprising. Above, different kinds of sausage, from Czechoslovakia, and drill bits from China. Right, a Hungarian label for the 1966 World Cup, and a Russian label commemorating the second world war battle for Volgograd.

(1983), Great Racing Cars (1984), Great American Cars, and History of the Aeroplane (1985). One well-known set of theirs, Angling, was 25 labels long and appeared in at least four varieties. Others included Wild West (two varieties), British Birds, Vintage Vehicles, Maynards Thru the Years, Speed Through the Ages, Military Uniforms, Chateaux of Bordeaux, Chateaux of the Loire, Wonders of the World and Vineyards of the World. Some of these labels were also reissued in Britain under the Duchy Match Co. brand.

In the post-war years, French labels were best known for their dullness once the production of matches there became a government monopoly. The ubiquitous grubby red-and – white 'Allumettes de Sûreté' displaced the 'Casque d'Or' (winged golden helmet on backgrounds of varying shades of green) label, variety only being provided by the occasional advertising labels. While the French government had established two substantial match factories it was still importing considerable quantities of matches from other European countries, as well as from Sweden.

By the 1960s French labels changed much for the better with the introduction of a colourful set of French provincial costumes, first lady's, then men's, in several styles and varieties. These were followed by

sets of fables, proverbs and regional house designs, regional proverbs and costumes combined, all colourful, bright and cheerful. A new road safety set was issued in 1971, and in the same year a set about space travel. The exploration of outer space was to be a popular label theme in many countries after Yuri Gagarin's first manned space flight in 1961. The Olympic Games and football World Cup also triggered off sets of match-box labels in countries all over

AVERAGE 50 CONTENTS

MADE IN FINLAND BY FINN-MATCH

DASCYLLUS AURUANUS

CATS
Series of 18 No. 5
Seal-point Siamese

Duchy Match Co.

Average Contents 48 Sticks

Made in Finland for Duchy Match Co.

Slim Pocket Size

ANGLING

The Cornish Match Co.

Made in Finland

50 AVERAGE CONTENTS

2P PER BOX

Series of 25 No 5 The Golden Carp

CATS
Series of 18 No. 2
Tortoiseshell-and-white
British Shorthair

The Cornish Match Co. Ltd.

Average Contents 45 Sticks

Made in Finland Exclusively for Finlay & Co. Ltd.

CATS
Series of 18 No. 17
Black Devon Rex

The Cornish Match Co. Ltd.

Average Contents 45 Sticks

Made in Finland Exclusively for Finlay & Co. Ltd.

Slim Pocket Size

ANGLING

The Cornish Match Co.

Made in Finland

45 AVERAGE CONTENTS

2P PER BOX

Series of 25 No 4 The Chub

CATS
Series of 18 No. 13
Blue-eyed white British
Shorthair

The Cornish Match Co. Ltd.

Average Contents 45 Sticks

Made in Finland Exclusively for Finlay & Co. Ltd.

Clockwise: one of a set of fish from Finn-Match for local distribution; cats from 1982 from Cornish Match (later Duchy Match Co.); and 'Angling' from the same company.

Top: popular 'Dog Breeds' set from Cornish Match (1980) and below, varieties of the numerous dog sets from the Yugoslavian Drava factory which first appeared in the 1960s.

Opposite page: Great Racing Cars set by the Cornish Match Co. for Lavells Newsagents (1984), and a Cornish Match label for Maynards (1982).

LAVELLS NEWSAGENTS *GREAT RACING CARS*

The Cornish Match Co. Ltd.

Made in Finland Av. 48 Sticks

Series of 18. No. 8 Alfa Romeo 1932

LAVELLS NEWSAGENTS *GREAT RACING CARS*

The Cornish Match Co. Ltd.

Made in Finland Av. 48 Sticks

Series of 18. No. 13 Lago — Talbot 1947

MAYNARDS Thru the Years

Average contents 48 Finnish Sticks

The Cornish Match Co. Ltd.

The Original-Still the Best *Maynards*

MAYNARD'S C?
180 Victoria St?
BRISTOL

Original WINE GUMS

circa 1925

Series of 18 No. 9

LAVELLS NEWSAGENTS *GREAT RACING CARS*

The Cornish Match Co. Ltd.

Made in Finland Av. 48 Sticks

Series of 18. No. 18 BRM 1970

LAVELLS NEWSAGENTS *GREAT RACING CARS*

The Cornish Match Co. Ltd.

Made in Finland Av. 48 Sticks

Series of 18. No. 1 Renault 1904

Series of 18 No 3 Cadillac V16 452B 1932

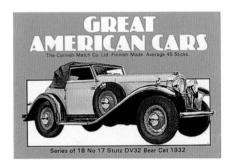

Series of 18 No 17 Stutz DV32 Bear Cat 1932

Series of 18 No 7 Dodge Sedan 1955

VINTAGE RAILWAY ENGINES

Great Eastern Railway. Locomotive 1855.
Series of 18 No 17

Made in Finland

The Cornish Match Co.

AVERAGE 52 CONTENTS

3P PER BOX

Series of 18 No 4 Chevrolet Nomad 1955

*Great American Cars' from the Cornish
Match Co., (1985) and a Vintage Railway
Engine from the same company.*

Made for Duchy Match Co
GREAT BRITISH CARS SERIES

DUCHY MATCH COMPANY

MADE IN FINLAND. AV. 48 STICKS

No 9 JAGUAR XK 120 1953-54

Made for Duchy Match Co
GREAT BRITISH CARS SERIES

DUCHY MATCH COMPANY

MADE IN FINLAND. AV. 48 STICKS

No 4 AUSTIN MINI-COOPER 1961-64

VINTAGE VEHICLES

MADE IN FINLAND

THE CORNISH MATCH CO. LTD.

50

3P

120 H.P. DE DIETRICH CAR
SERIES OF 18 No 6

Made for Duchy Match Co
GREAT BRITISH CARS SERIES

DUCHY MATCH COMPANY

MADE IN FINLAND. AV. 48 STICKS

No 7 BRISTOL 401 1949-53

VINTAGE
RAILWAY ENGINES

Made in Finland

The Cornish Match Co.

52
AVERAGE CONTENTS

3P
PER BOX

Caledonian Railway. Locomotive 903.
Series of 18 No 11

*'Great British Cars' (1981);
'Vintage Vehicles' and 'Vintage
Railway Engines'.*

sets appeal 153

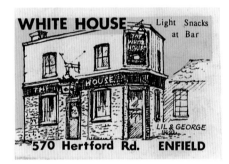

ST. PETERS – JERSEY

BOULDENS MATCH Co. Southampton   FOREIGN MATCHES

Pubs and pub signs generated some of the longest-known sets of British matchbox labels.

Opposite page: Russian imports of the era included Chestnut, County Pride (1954) and Scottish Heather (1954).

the world whenever they took place, and true to form during this era France produced a set for the Mexico Olympics.

With an intensifying struggle for market share which saw conglomerates competing against independent distributors, and global factories vying with each other for export customers – all facing an increase in the use of disposable lighters, free advertising matchbooks and boxes and a decline in smoking – the sourcing of cheaper, reliable matches was ever-important to distributors with already slim profit margins. Even the giant Bryant & May company, once a backbone of the industry, closed two of its three remaining British factories as part of its diversification programme in the 1970s. By 1981 only their Merseyside plant was still making matches – the only one in the country, eventually closing down in 1994.

As the independents continued producing sets of labels, and importing from varied sources, the only real beneficiaries were label collectors who were able to enjoy the last real surge of label output before they became increasingly replaced by the continuous-process cardboard skillet. Nevertheless some of the sets described here continued to appear in the new format, as printed boxes.

Germany was to be the source of matches for a set of twelve Sussex Castles produced by the Sussex Match Co. The Duchy Match Co. used German matches for their Historic Cornwall set, while Solo Match (UK) issued Rhine Castles and aircraft sets.

Hungary was a further origin of imported matches, albeit briefly, providing the contents for the Anglo Austrian Match Co's. set of 20 'Riddles of Yesterday' labels in 1968. Soon after, the export of matches from Hungary to Britain was suspended.

For several years Italy had been exporting an attractive set entitled

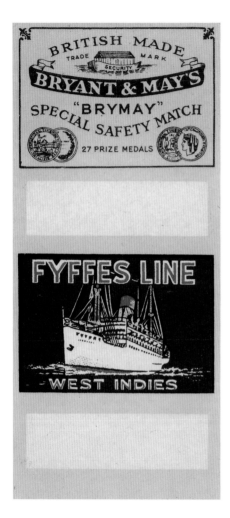

'Folklore Scenes', initially identified as being of Italian origin, but later under the 'Foreign Made' banner. Nine different varieties of this set are known to exist. The Southern Counties Match co. used Italian matches for two sets in the late 1980s. The first, in 1988, was actually a combination of ten sets, totalling 198 labels featuring Royal Navy badges. These labels were unusual in that they also carried a message encouraging buyers to 'collect the ten sets of badges in this series of 198 labels.' The company went on to issue a set of forty-two labels entitled 'The World Goes to War' the following year. Previously, Southern Counties Match Co.had also bought matches from Latvia for their 1979 sixty-long British Military Uniforms set, and for their 'Last Steam Locomotives of the World', oddly-numbered at fifty-seven.

The Drava factory in Osijeck, the largest in former Yugoslavia, was already successful in exporting its products, not only to other Balkan countries but to Austria, Germany, Switzerland, Holland, North and South America and elsewhere. It was among the first to compete in the set scramble in the British market with its well-known dogs series. Initially released in the 1960s, the first set of ten labels grew to 24 and exists in half-a-dozen varieties. It continued to be issued for almost 30 years. The Two Counties Match Co. also sold Yugoslavian matches via their 'Ten Country Scenes'set.

While not a major exporter, Holland's match industry was sustained by a surprisingly strong domestic market and produced an abundance of labels for a relatively small country. During the 1960s and 1970s output was particularly prolific, producing some well-known sets featuring both traditional and (then) modern subjects.

Covering about ten years from the mid-1960s to mid-1970s, the Mode series featured female fashion trends. Another series with a 'swinging sixties' feel featured film and pop stars of the era in about six different sets, totalling several hundred different labels – although some of the biggest stars appear more than once.

Probably the best known is the famous Dutch windmill set. Developed from the original single 'Molen Lucifers' label, which itself appeared in a number of varieties over the early years of its production, it blossomed into a colourful set depicting windmills from all over the Netherlands, totalling 360 in number.

Russia was always a big player in match exports, and Russian matches

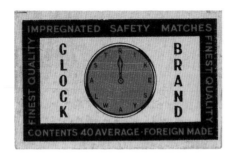

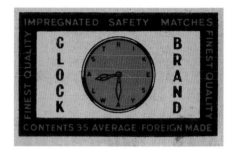

Believed to number almost 900 varieties, the Russian 'Clock' brand label first appeared in 1951.

have been available in the Middle East, North Africa, many European countries and even the USA, variously labelled as 'Made in Russia', 'Made in USSR', or 'Foreign Made'. The British market has sold countless Russian brands, either in single label form or in sets. Among the earlier Russian labels to be seen in Britain were The Regular (about 1914), Thistle (1921), and Heroical (1934), but it was to be the 1950s that witnessed a significant rise in Russian imports. Brands such as Criterion and Paramount were common, and although originally registered in 1929 both brands flourished in the 1950s. Others were Tulip (1950), County Pride and Scottish (sometimes Scotch) Heather (1954), The Trident (1955}, Prestige (1958), and Fire Queen (1959). In later years Britannia Match Co. was to issue a pretty set of birds, and Essex Match a set of twelve Helicopters of the World, both using matches of USSR origin.

Even Switzerland was to contribute

to the dilution of sales by the big conglomerates. As early as 1935 the Kandergrund factory had begun issuing sets of picturesque views of Switzerland, boxes which proved very popular with tourists over the following years and which helped sustain domestic sales. In 1966 and 1968 two new updated sets of ten labels each were released, and in 1971 a new set of 24 scenes was issued, exported to Britain and distributed by Britannia Match Co. who released four sets in the mid to late 1970s. The other Swiss factory, Etincelle AG, also issued and exported a set of twenty labels of their own at about the same time.

Swiss matches were used by the Southern Counties Match Co. for one of their Steam Locomotives of the World sets, and Yorkshire Match Co. drew upon Swiss stock for yet another scenery-inspired set, this one entitled Yorkshire Scenes.

At a time when major match companies were struggling to sustain

TOURIST ZÜNDHÖLZER

Sicherheitshölzer
Allumettes de sûreté

TRUSTFREIE
ZÜNDWARENFABRIK
KANDERGRUND

Neuchâtel

Made in Switzerland   Avge. cont. 40 safety matches

Luzern

Made in Switzerland   Avge. cont. 40 safety matches

RHINE CASTLES   No. 9

SOLO MATCHES (UK) LIMITED   MADE IN W. GERMANY - 40 CONTENTS

BURG PFALZ

RHINE CASTLES   No. 11

SOLO MATCHES (UK) LIMITED   MADE IN W. GERMANY - 40 CONTENTS

BURG RHEINSTEIN

Schilthorn Mürren

Made in Switzerland   Avge. cont. 40 safety matches

LAST STEAM LOCOMOTIVES OF THE WORLD   NO 19

CONTENTS 40 SWISS MATCHES   TEL. 0202 741885

Send S.A.E. for details of Special Wall Chart Offer
Photos By Colin Garratt ©

SOUTHERN COUNTIES MATCH CO. POOLE

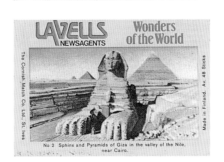

LAVELLS NEWSAGENTS   Wonders of the World

The Cornish Match Co. Ltd., St. Ives.   Made in Finland. Av. 48 Sticks

No. 2 Sphinx and Pyramids of Giza in the valley of the Nile, near Cairo.

The old 'Tourist' label from the Swiss Kandergrund factory perhaps inspired these later Swiss Scenes labels (1966). 'Rhine Castles', 'Wonders of the World' and 'Last Steam Locomotives of the World' were other common sets of the time.

'British Military Uniforms' by Southern Counties Match Co. (1979).

sales, the simultaneous blossoming of so many regional importers and distributors providing between them such a variety of product, and investing so much money to enable them to do so, was surprising. Not so surprising was the ultimate result; not enough market share for everyone, and, inevitably sales figures which continued on an irrevocable downward path.

The increase in the importation of and distribution of foreign matches did little to generate sales volumes – but it did provide more variety of choice for the customer.

The description 'Foreign Made' on matchbox labels goes back to about 1920, when it first appeared as a result of a requirement to identify the country of origin on imported matches which was introduced in 1914. When it was not politically desirable to specifically name the country of origin, importers made do with 'Foreign Made' – at least until the end of 1972 when the ruling was relaxed. A few variations on the theme included 'British Empire Made' and 'Made in Europe'.

During this time many 'Foreign Made' brands appeared in British and other markets. One of these, Clock Brand, was to become one of the longest sets of labels ever issued. Imported from Russia between about

169 Wip-watermolen Breukelen (U.)

MOLEN LUCIFERS

161 Korenmolen Den Oever (N.H.)

MOLEN LUCIFERS

17 Wipwatermolen te Hoogmade

MOLEN LUCIFERS

1951 and 1972, Clock Brand match-boxes featured a clock face on the label, each new issue showing the time changed by fifteen minutes. In three different sizes, two types of printing ('fat' hand size and 'thin'), eleven different contents sizes making about 18 different sets, the number of different Clock labels is believed to be about 866.

The longest set of all? Pub labels were always abundant, produced in their hundreds by independent companies like Bouldens, Wessex Match and the ubiquitous Cornish Match

Co. The longest set is probably the one produced for Whitbreads Brewery, believed to number 960 in total.

This is by no means a complete list of all the sets issued during this competitive era, nor of all the companies or countries that entered combat. There can probably never be a complete catalogue, but this is at least an insight to the state of trade at the time.

84 Gesloten standerdmolen Nistelrode (N-Br.)

MOLEN LUCIFERS

Popular among collectors: the famous Dutch windmills set which numbers 360 labels.

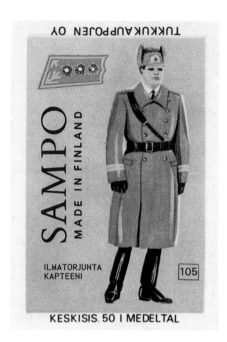

SAMPO MADE IN FINLAND

ILMATORJUNTA KAPTEENI

105

KESKISIS. 50 I MEDELTAL

TUKKUKAUPPOJEN OY

SAMPO MADE IN FINLAND

TYKISTÖ-ALIKERSANTTI PALVELUSPUVUSSA

50

KESKISIS. 50 I MEDELTAL

TUKKUKAUPPOJEN OY

THE WORLD GOES TO WAR. 1939-1945
50th ANNIVERSARY

LEST WE FORGET

Southern Counties Match Co. Poole (0202) 671172   Collect the complete set of 42.   No.11

IMPREGNATED FOR SAFETY

THE TRIDENT

SAFETY MATCH

REGD. TRADE MARK

MADE IN U.S.S.R.   AVERAGE CONTENTS 32

THE BRITANNIA MATCH CO. LONDON

Military themes from Finland and Southern Counties Match Co., who issued 'Royal Navy Badges' in 1988 and 'The World Goes to War' the following year. 'Trident' was a Russian import for Britannia Match Co.

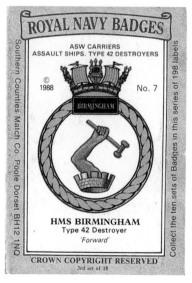

ROYAL NAVY BADGES

ASW CARRIERS
ASSAULT SHIPS. TYPE 42 DESTROYERS

© 1988   No. 7

BIRMINGHAM

HMS BIRMINGHAM
Type 42 Destroyer
'Forward'

'CROWN COPYRIGHT RESERVED'
3rd set of 18

Southern Counties Match Co. Poole Dorset BH12 1NQ   Collect the ten sets of Badges in this series of 198 labels

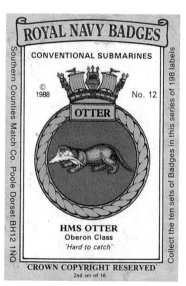

ROYAL NAVY BADGES

CONVENTIONAL SUBMARINES

© 1988   No. 12

OTTER

HMS OTTER
Oberon Class
'Hard to catch'

'CROWN COPYRIGHT RESERVED'
2nd set of 16

Southern Counties Match Co. Poole Dorset BH12 1NQ   Collect the ten sets of Badges in this series of 198 labels

Common Russian imports such as Fire Queen, Paramount, Criterion and Prestige flourished in the 1950s and 60s. 'Helicopters of the World' first came in 1987. Boxed sets were popular with tourists in the USSR.

23 Natalie Wood

22 Cliff Richard

C 10 Mick Jagger

16 Brigitte Bardot

Marianne Faithfull

*Pop stars, movie stars and
fashion feature on these
Dutch labels from the
swinging 'sixties.*

VLINDER

63 Elvis Presley

UITG. '71-'72 NR. 9

11 '70

NED. FAB.

Chapter Fourteen

Disappearing by Design:
The Matchbox Makeover

The design of these modern 'familiari' matches from Italy is in stark contrast with the detailed artwork of the match girl selling R.Bell & Co.'s Royal Wax Vestas in the late 19th century.

The last quarter of the twentieth century saw matchbox design take on a whole new face, particularly in Western Europe and North America.

In these 'modern' markets the proliferation of commercially-oriented collectors' sets, advertising and customers own-brand labels inevitably led to the replacement of those imaginative and colourful designs of the first part of the century by stock photography and company logos. The process was rapidly accelerated by the introduction of the cardboard skillet, particularly in the USA, one of the first countries to witness the virtual disappearance of the traditional wooden matchbox.

Nevertheless there are still plenty of parts of the world where labels are glued to matchboxes in the old way, and which carry their colourful messages among the population. While these may be declining, they continue to be a source of inspiration and information to collectors and historians alike.

Long silent now are the cries of London's match girls and the street vendors of the big cities of a century ago. Silent too are the great factories of Bow and Glasgow and 100 other places, and the countless small factories that burnt down or sold up.

Gone is the glimmer of gaslight from the lamps of the world's avenues and the drawing rooms of gentlefolk, from the candles of the more humble, and the means of lighting them: the fusees, vesuvians, congreves, pullmatches and other ingenious firemaking devices, all extinguished.

The matchbox has seen the transition from paper wrapper, wooden cylinder or pillbox to matchwood box and tray bound and glued with paper, then labelled. Then to labelled, cardboard boxes, then to the printed card box we know today, and in an astonishing variety of styles and sizes. Fliptops and barrels, minis and midgets and extra long cigar splints are all available as promotional items, competing still with dispos-

able lighters and match books.

Commercial rather than social, their messages are nonetheless often colourful and varied thanks to modern materials and production methods. But today the standard box of matches, if not produced by one of the household name brands, is likely to be simply decorated – if at all – or to have the distributor's name or logo on one side. The other side will typically be cluttered with bar code, E number, BS number, country of origin, contents, importer's name and address, and quality guarantee. They also now carry environmental and safety messages, such as 'sulphurless matches', 'environmentally safe', 'store in a dry place', 'keep away from children' and instructions for use such as 'strike softly away from body'. The messages are beginning to look familiar.

There will always be a need for matches. Man, the naked ape, will always need the naked flame, and still the international conglomerates manufacture and distribute high-quality wooden matches across much of the world. The packaging has changed, as has communication. Rural match factories still produce colourful and informative labels for local consumption, and still collectors track down and discover old boxes and labels, often intact and well preserved after a century or more.

The matchbox label has provided a fascinating pictorial insight and reference to social history, to fashion, transport, lifestyle, consumerism and countless other topics for over a 150 years. As long as matches are made and used daily by ordinary people throughout the world, they will remain a barometer of social activity and, hopefully, a means of communication and source of information, both for today and for the future.

The printed matchbox of today (above) is often cluttered with barcodes and safety information, while the early wax vestas box of 150 years ago is elegantly simple – and the 'little girl with sulphur matches' is no longer with us.

Opposite page: Toys in matchboxes.

MILESTONE
IMPREGNATED

2½D

AVERAGE
48
MATCHES

SAFETY MATCHES

MADE IN ITALY

Chapter Fifteen

Matchbox Milestones

Opposite page: Milestone. Imported from Italy and first registered in 1926, this version dates from about 1960.

Above: USSR, 1935.

1827: John Walker's 'Friction Lights' go on sale – the world's first.

1833: Match production starts in Italy at the Albani factory.

1835: Balthazar Mertens starts making matches in Belgium.

1836: In the USA Alonzo Philips produces his 'first improved friction matches'.

1836: First Swedish match factory established by J.S.Bagge.

1837: First Russian match factory starts operation near St. Petersburg.

1840: Pascasio Lizarbe Ruis opens Spain's first match factory.

1840: Finland's first match factory starts production.

1843: Britain's Bryant & May is established.

1846: Match manufacture begins in Norway.

1862: US Congress introduces a match tax as part of the Revenue Act.

1871: British Chancellor of the Exchequer Robert Lowe proposes introduction of a match tax. The proposal is rapidly withdrawn after a public outcry.

1871: In Australia, the 'first match manufactory in the Colonies' opens in North Richmond, Victoria.

1876: Captain Matthew Webb becomes the first person to swim the English channel, inspiring the eponymous match brand.

1880: Diamond Match Co. is founded in USA.

1884: Match production starts in South Africa.

1884: The three-week match girls strike at Bryant & May's Fairfield Works in Bow, London, ends, resulting in the establishment of the first trade union for women.

1892: Joshua Pusey patents the book match in the USA.

1895: Ohio Match Co. founded in the USA.

1903: Austrian independent match companies merge to form Solo AG.

1904: In Brazil the Fiat Lux match company starts production.

1905: Foundation of the Philippine Match Co.

1912: Union Allumettière (Union

171

Indian independence, 1947 and below right, the 1948 'Jubileums' label celebrated Jönköpings' 100th year of production.

Opposite page: Promotional sales material for the Norwegian Nitedals factory shows a wide range of their brands and dates from before 1915, when the Red Cross brand was withdrawn Right: matches on boxes. Three prewar Belgian examples.

Match) founded in Belgium.

1913: Bryant & May acquire S & J Moreland of Gloucester.

1915: Chile's major match company, Cia. Chileana de Fósforos, is founded.

1917: Merger of major Swedish match companies to form Svenska Tändsticks AB: Swedish Match.

1924: Opening of Nur match factory in Acre, Palestine.

1930: First Egyptian match factory established.

1932: Suicide of Ivar Kreuger, the Swedish 'Match King', who financed and controlled much of the world's match industry.

1935: 'Heroical' and 'Help' brands are issued in Russia to celebrate the rescue of the crew of the Chelyushkin Polar exploration ship.

1935: Establishment of SEITA, the French match monopoly.

1939: Great China Match Co. starts production in Hong Kong.

1945: British Matchbox Label & Booklet Society founded.

1947: Independence of India sees issue of many celebratory labels in that country.

1948: Jönköpings match factory issues 'Jubileums' label to celebrate 100 years of production at their Lake Vättern factory,

1959: The Swan on the vesta box changes direction and swims from left to right. It still does.

1973: Bryant & May merge with Wilkinson Sword and create Wilkinson Match.

1979: Wilkinson Match close their London factory.

1980: Wilkinson Match sells to Allegheny International.

1981: New owners close former Bryant & May Glasgow factory.

1987: Swedish Match acquire the match manufacturing interests of Allegheny International.

1994: Match production in Britain ceases with the closure of the former Bryant & May factory in Liverpool.

1996: Bryant & May cease trading. Operations continue as Swedish Match-and all over the world Royal weddings, coronations and jubilees, major sporting events and achievements of national or international importance have been commemorated on matchbox labels.

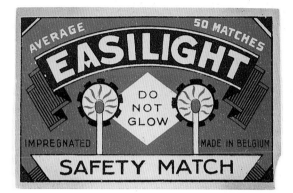

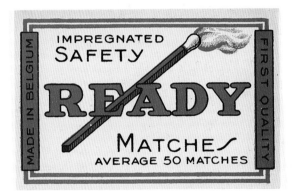

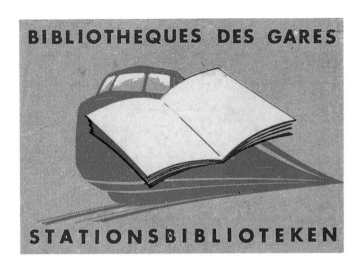

BIBLIOTHEQUES DES GARES

STATIONSBIBLIOTEKEN

Belgian label promoting station bookshops.

Opposite: 'Index' – a popular Italian import from 1950. Other versions of this label first appeared in 1925.

Bibliography

Beaver, Patrick:
The Matchmakers;
Henry Melland, London,
1985

Cruse, A.J.:
Match-Box Labels of the World,
Robert Ross, London,
1946

Loewe, Walter; Jonsson, Arne; Rossell, Carl Magnus:
From Swedish Matches to Swedish Match;
Wahlstrom & Widstrand, Stockholm, 1997

Rendell, Joan:
Collecting Matchbox Labels;
Arco, London, 1963

Rendell, Joan:
Matchbox Labels;
David & Charles,
Newton Abbott, 1968

Rendell, Joan:
The Match, The Box and The Label; David & Charles,
Newton Abbott, 1983

Specialist Publications;

Tejder, Arne:
Swedish Match Factories;
Gothenberg, 1978

Van der Plank, David & Rosemarie: *The Match Label Collector's Handbook,*
St.Ives, 1972

Periodicals:
Vesta (May1977-April 1987)

Match Label News
British Matchbox Label and Booklet Society.
122 High Street,
Melbourn,
Cambs. SG8 6AL

Index